Vintage Book Collage Art
By Jolie Ruin

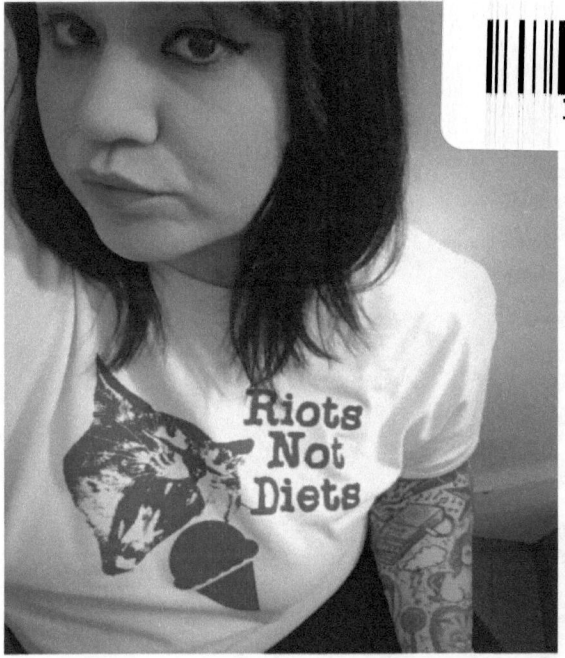

I'm Jolie. I make collages. This book contains a lot of my collage art that I have created with vintage books and magazines,mostly from the 1940s and 1950s. The collages were all made in 2017 and 2018.

Find me on social media as JolieRuin
I sell art, zines and t-shirts on Etsy:
TheEscapistArtist.Etsy.Com
I also run the new Riot Grrrl Press.

Riot Grrrl Press 2018

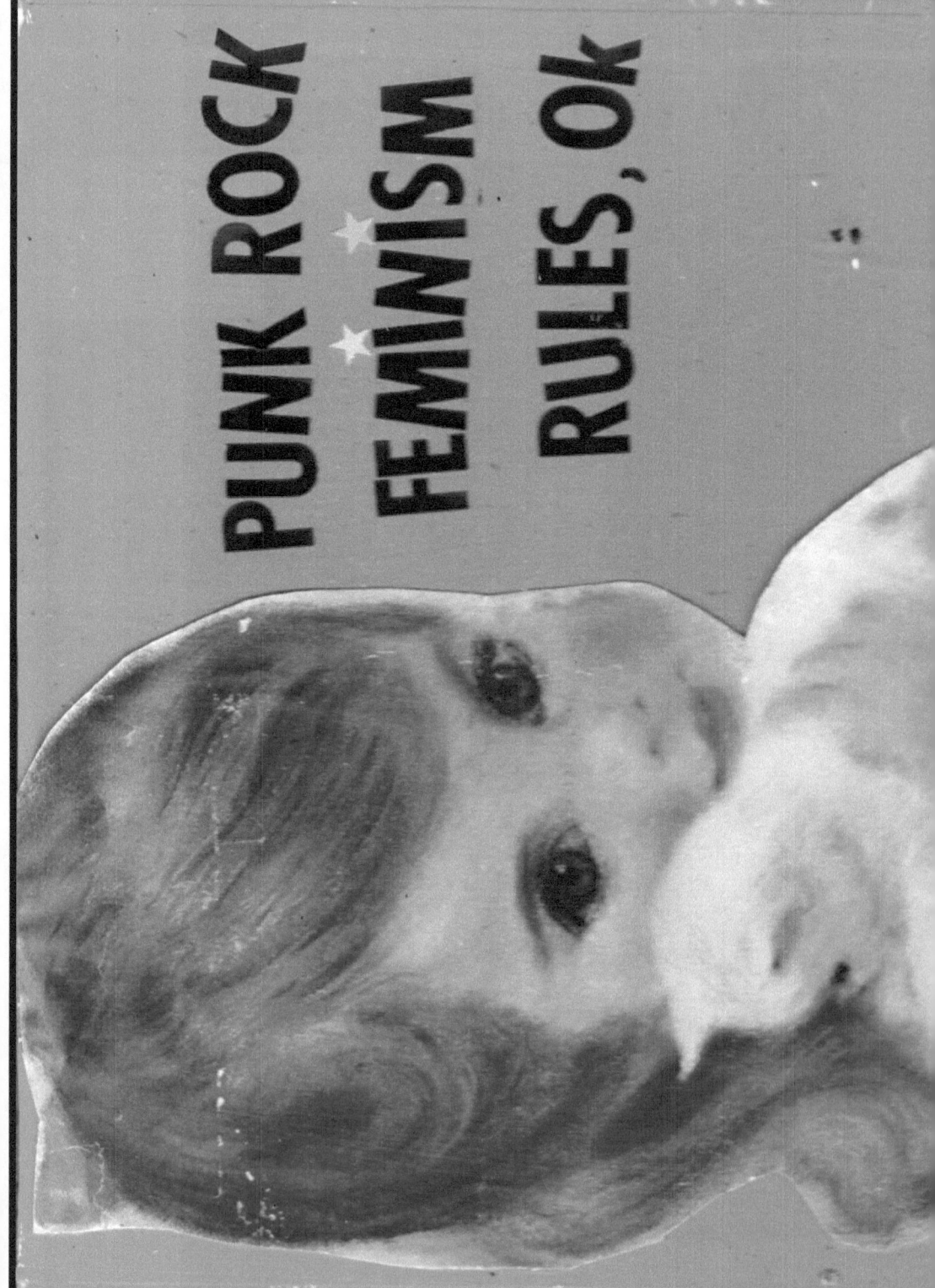

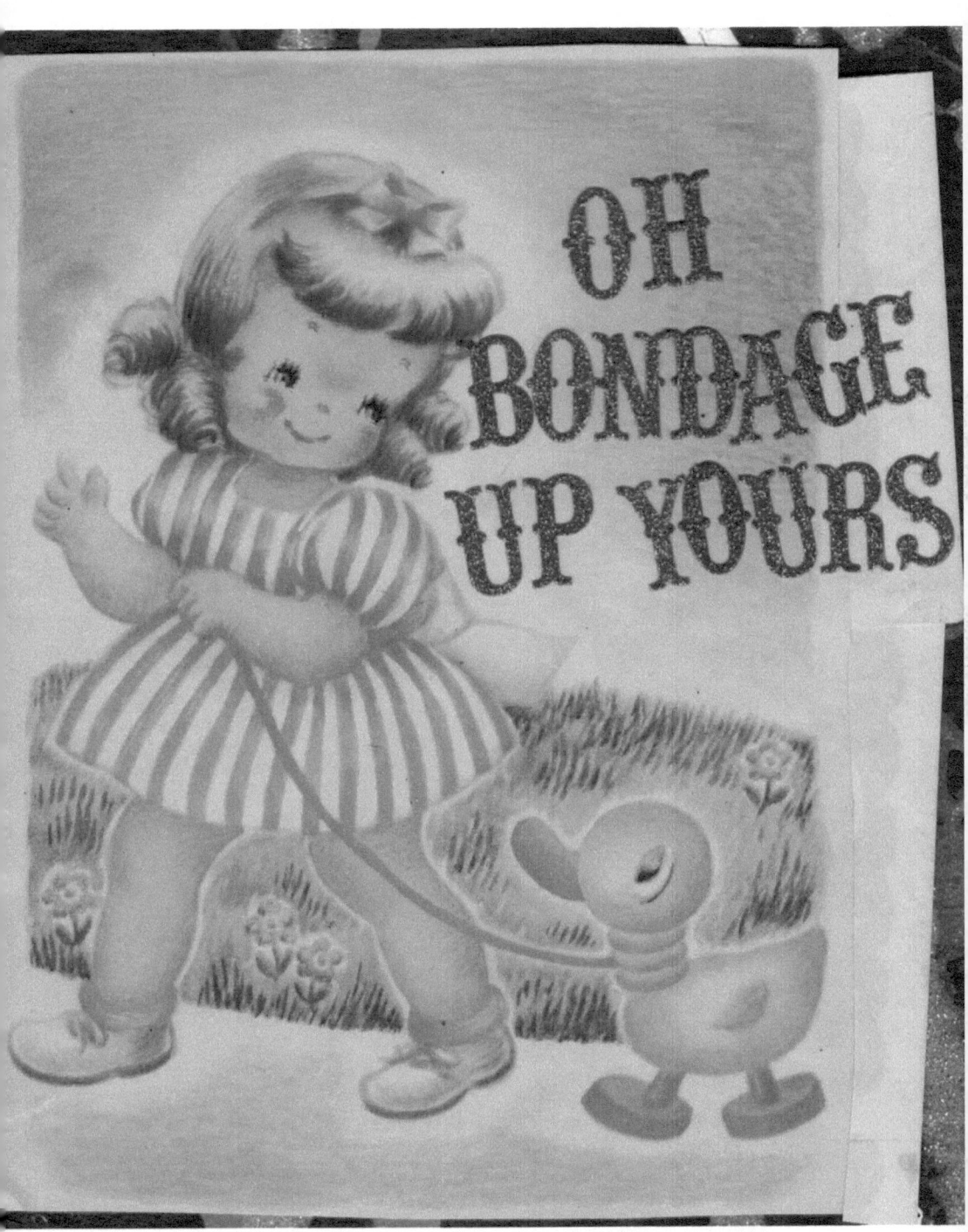

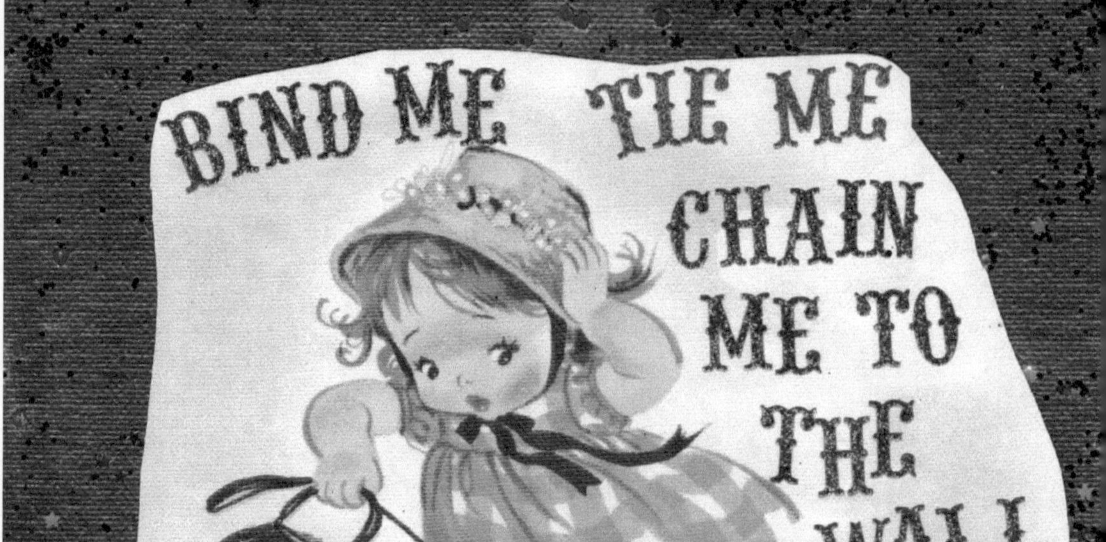
BIND ME TIE ME
CHAIN
ME TO
THE
WALL

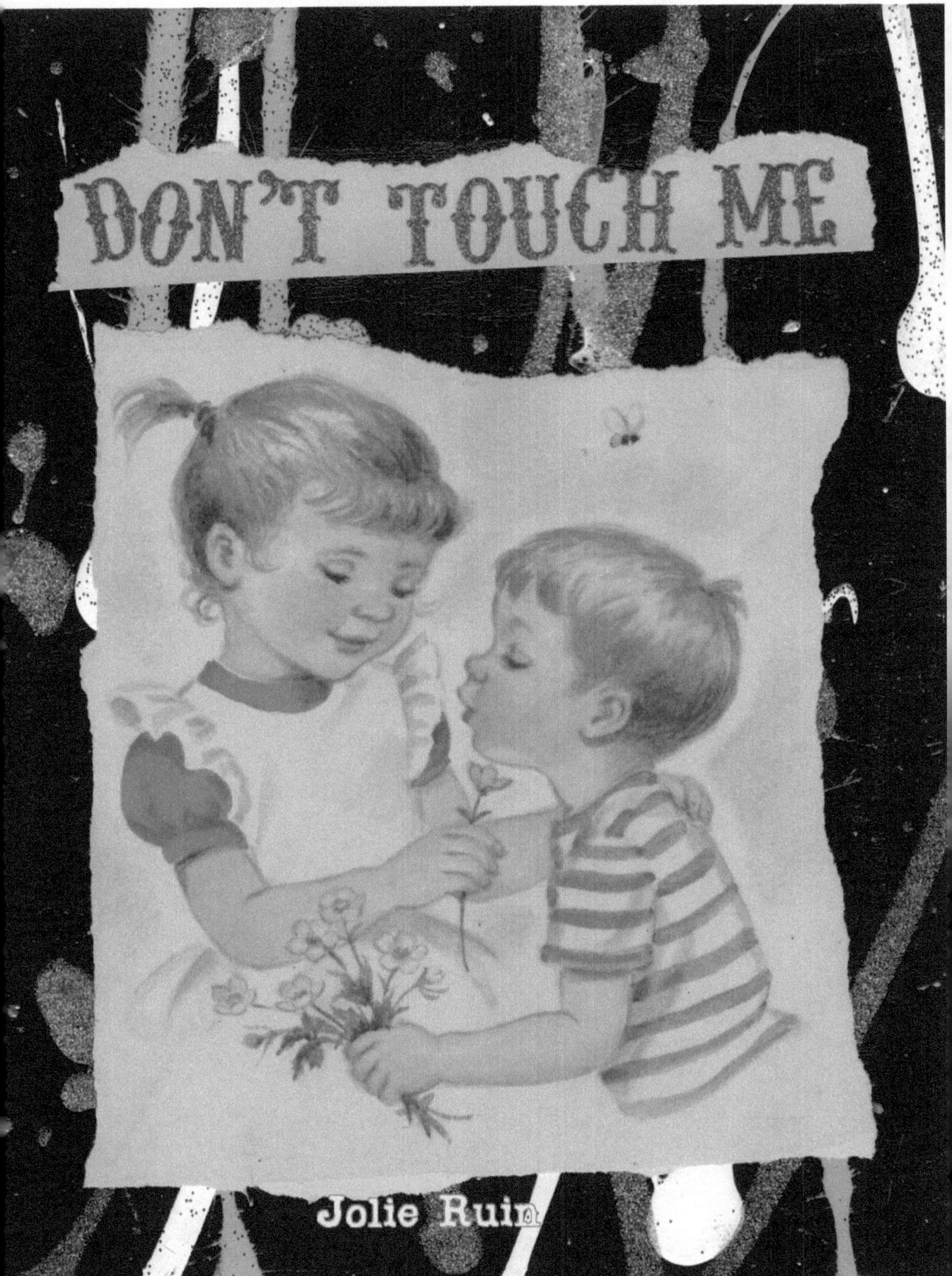
DON'T TOUCH ME
Jolie Ruin

I HOPE YOU DIE

Jolie Ruin

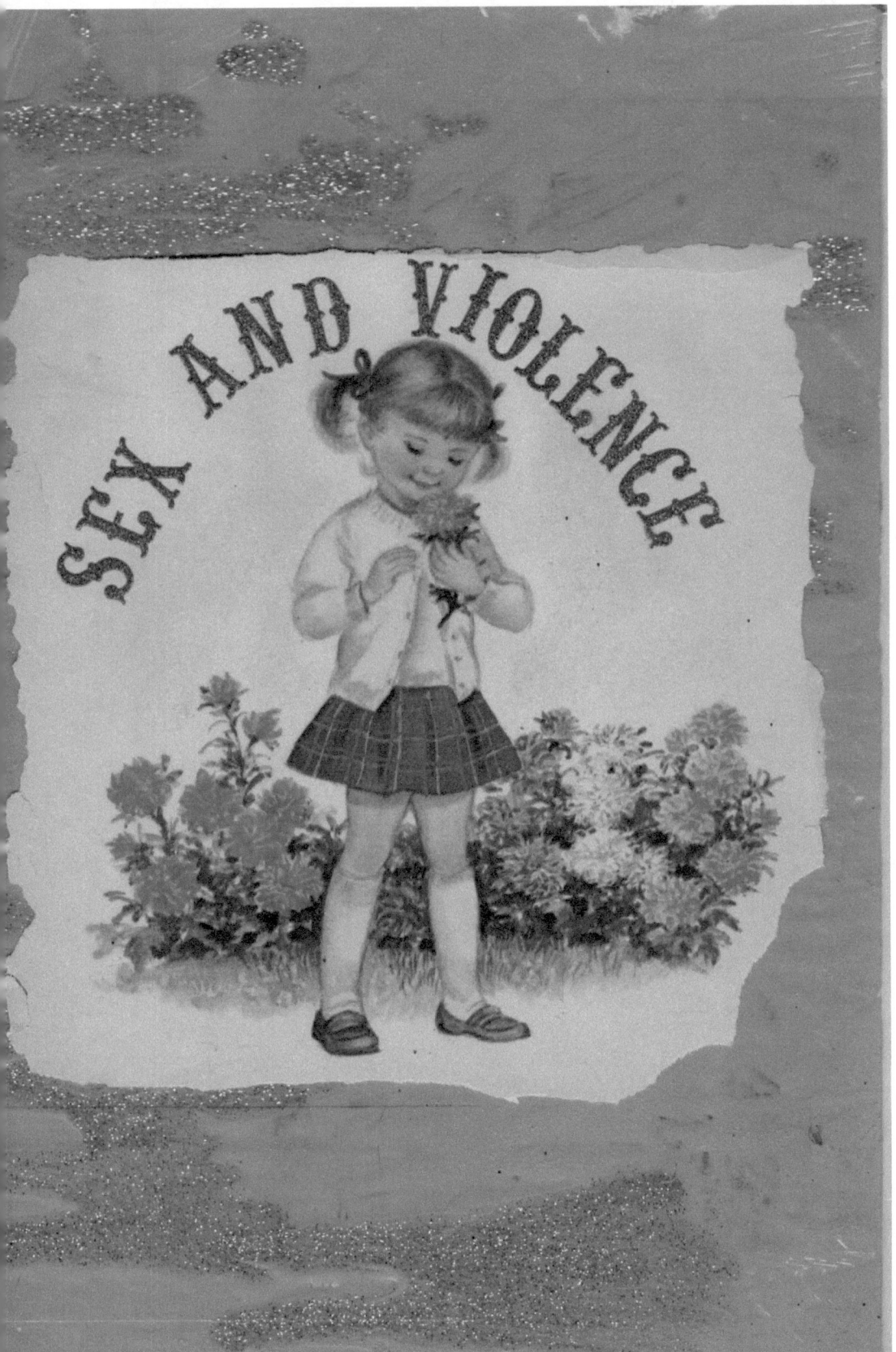

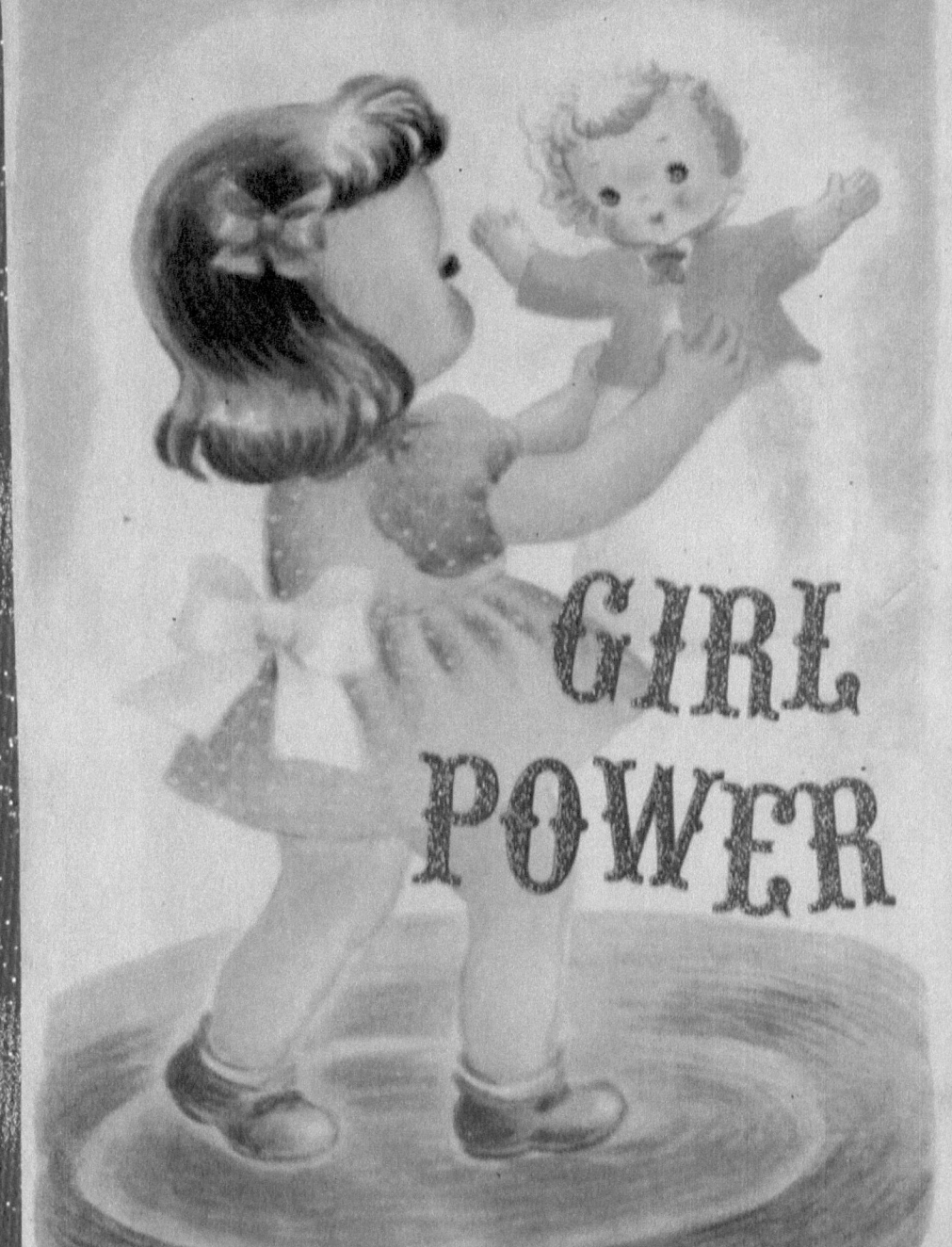

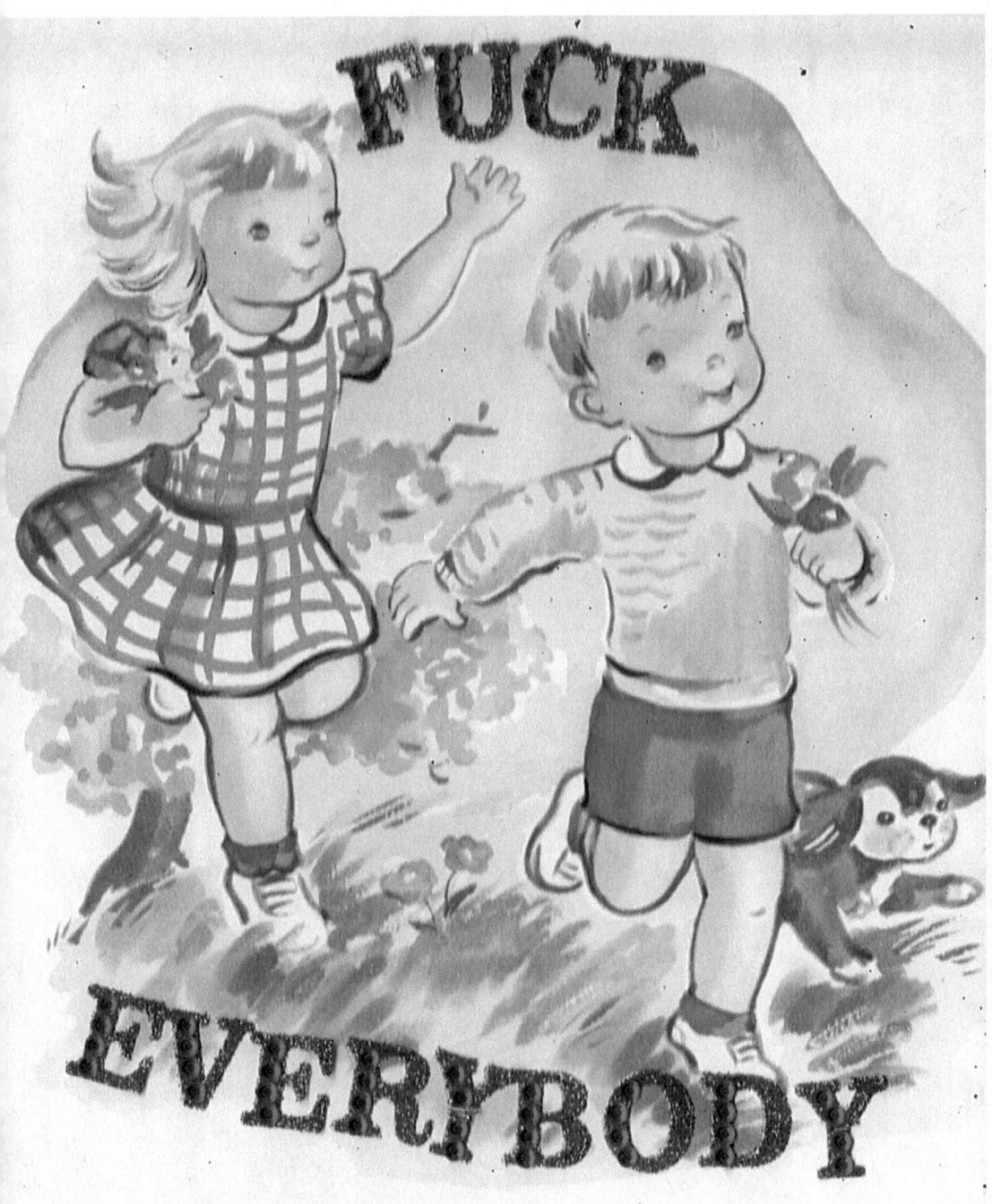

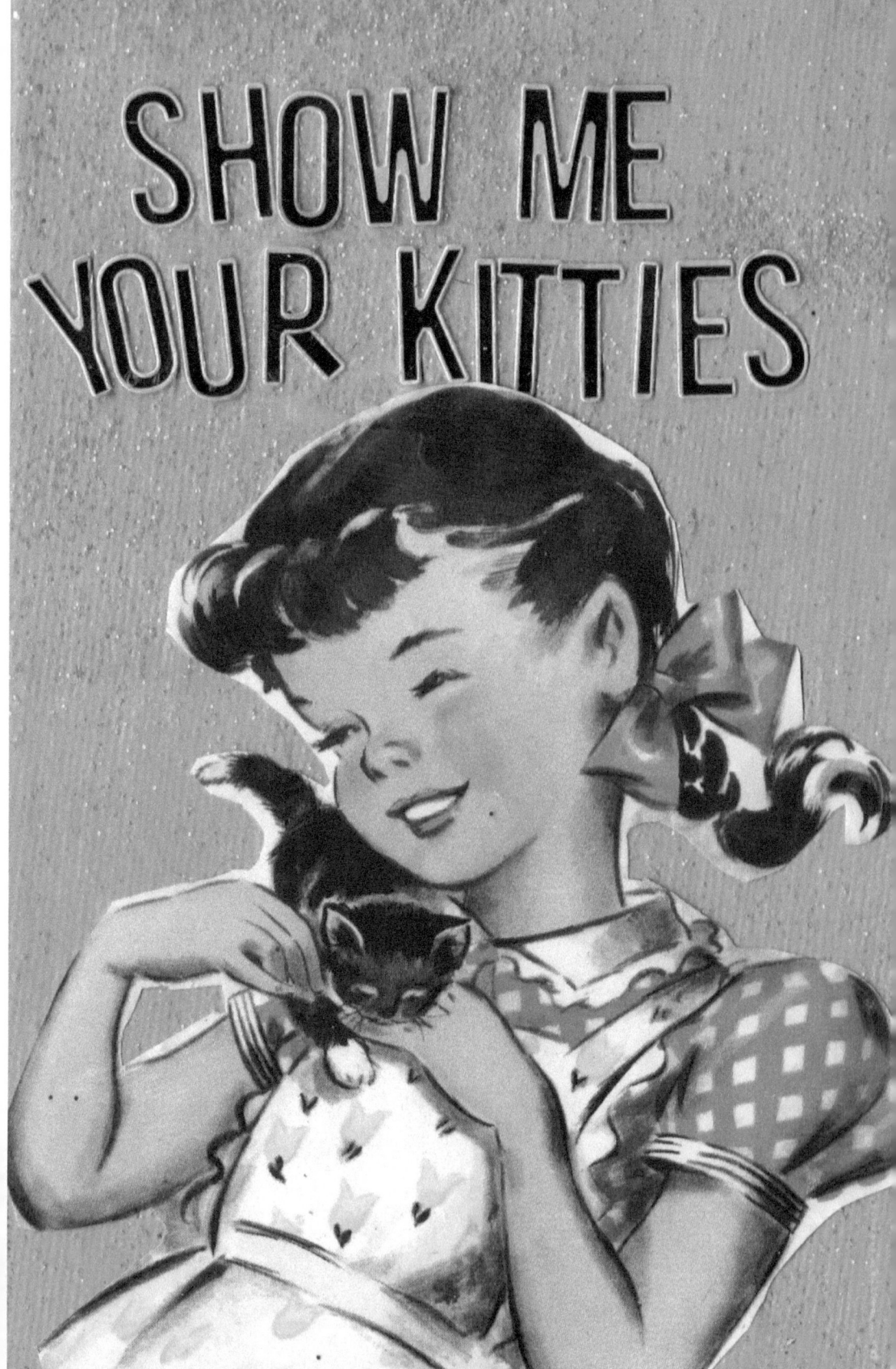

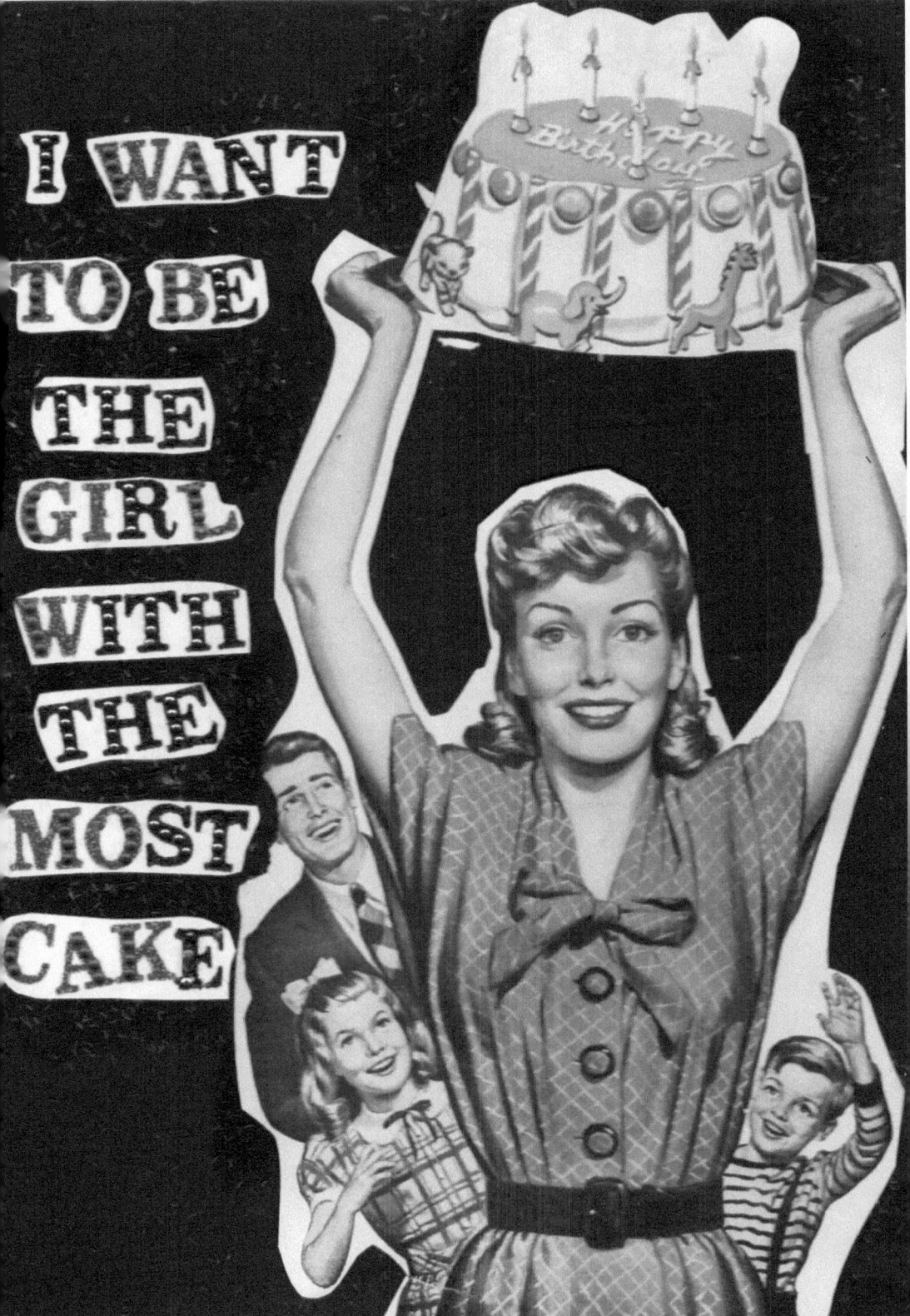

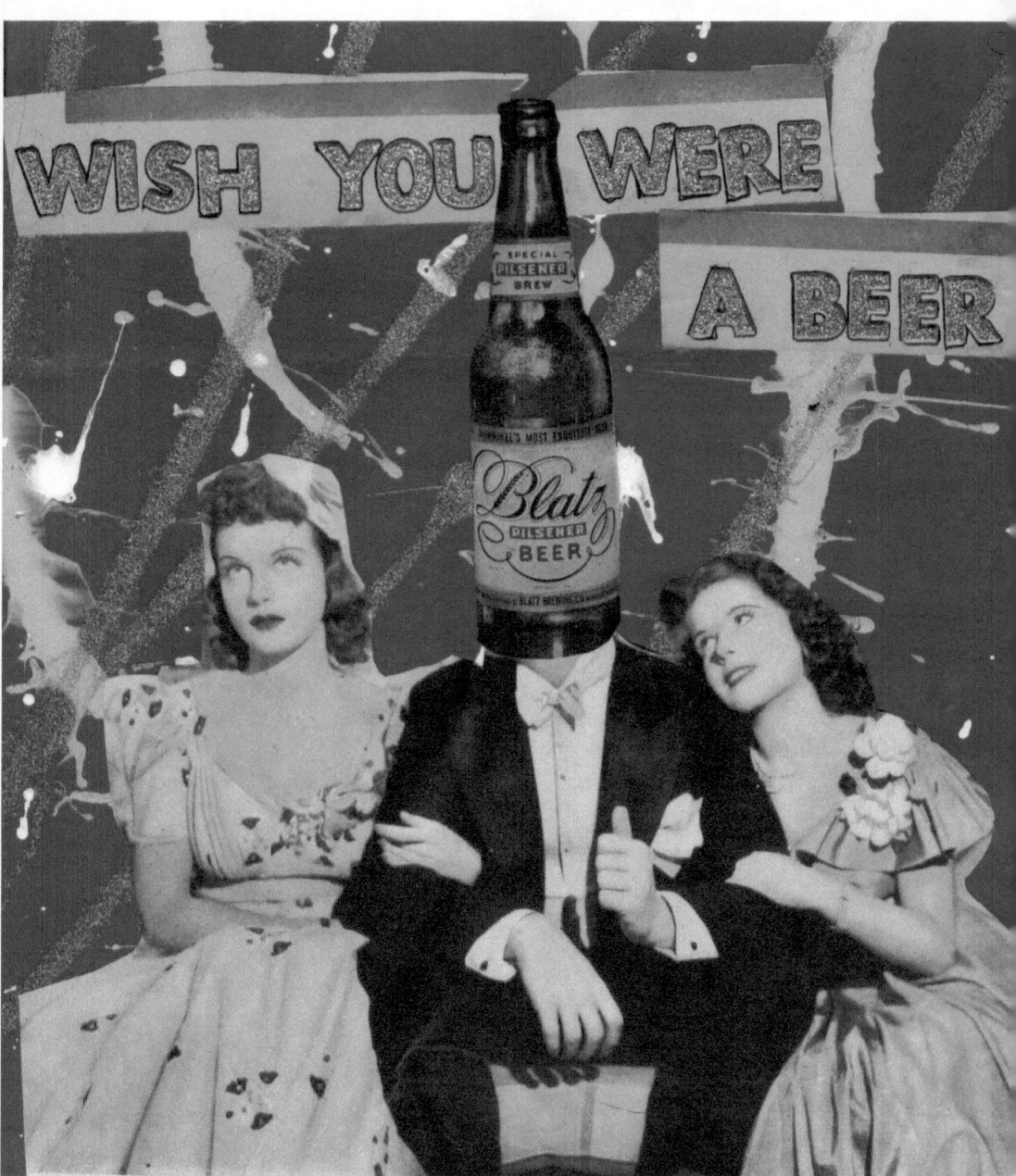

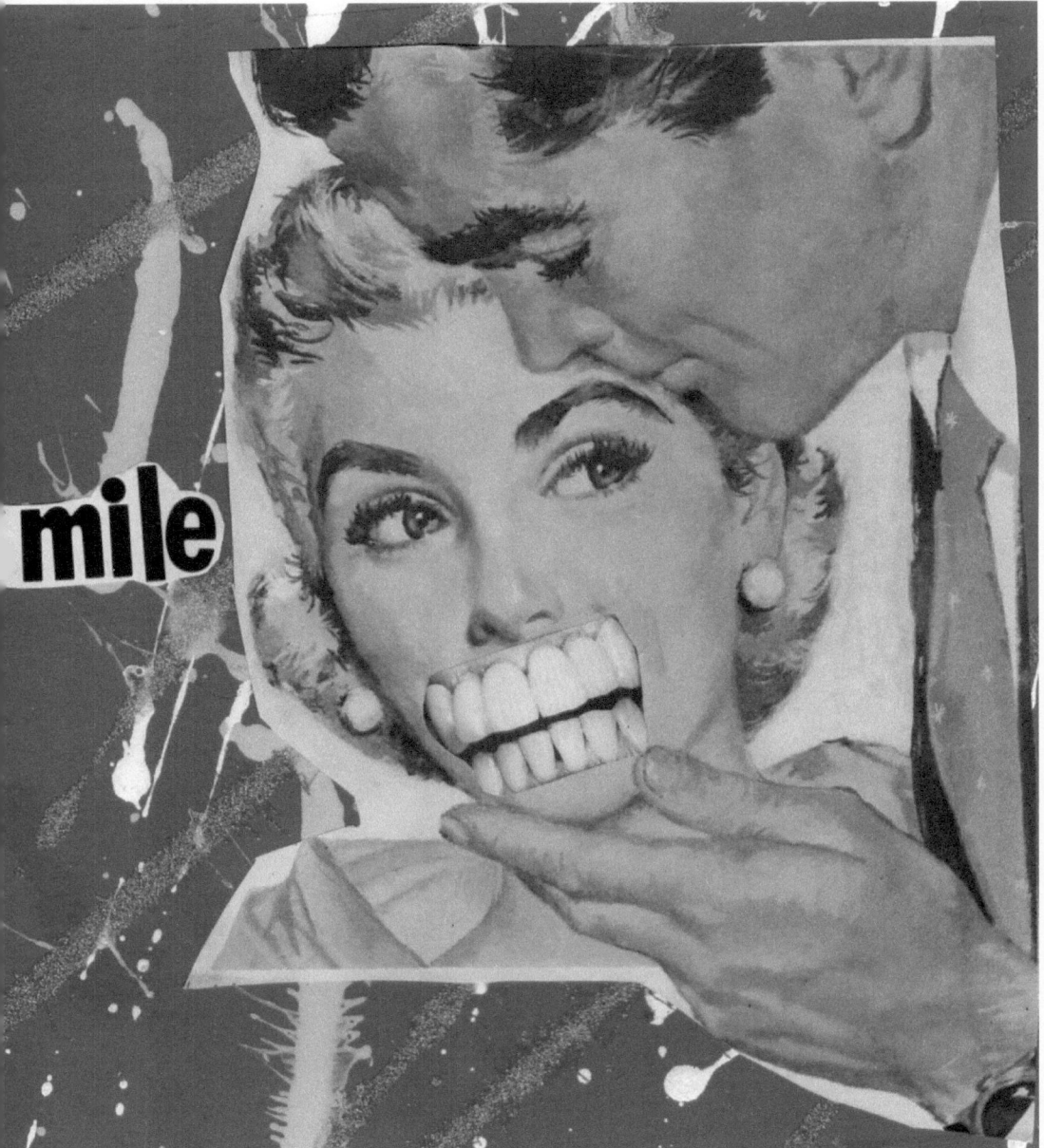

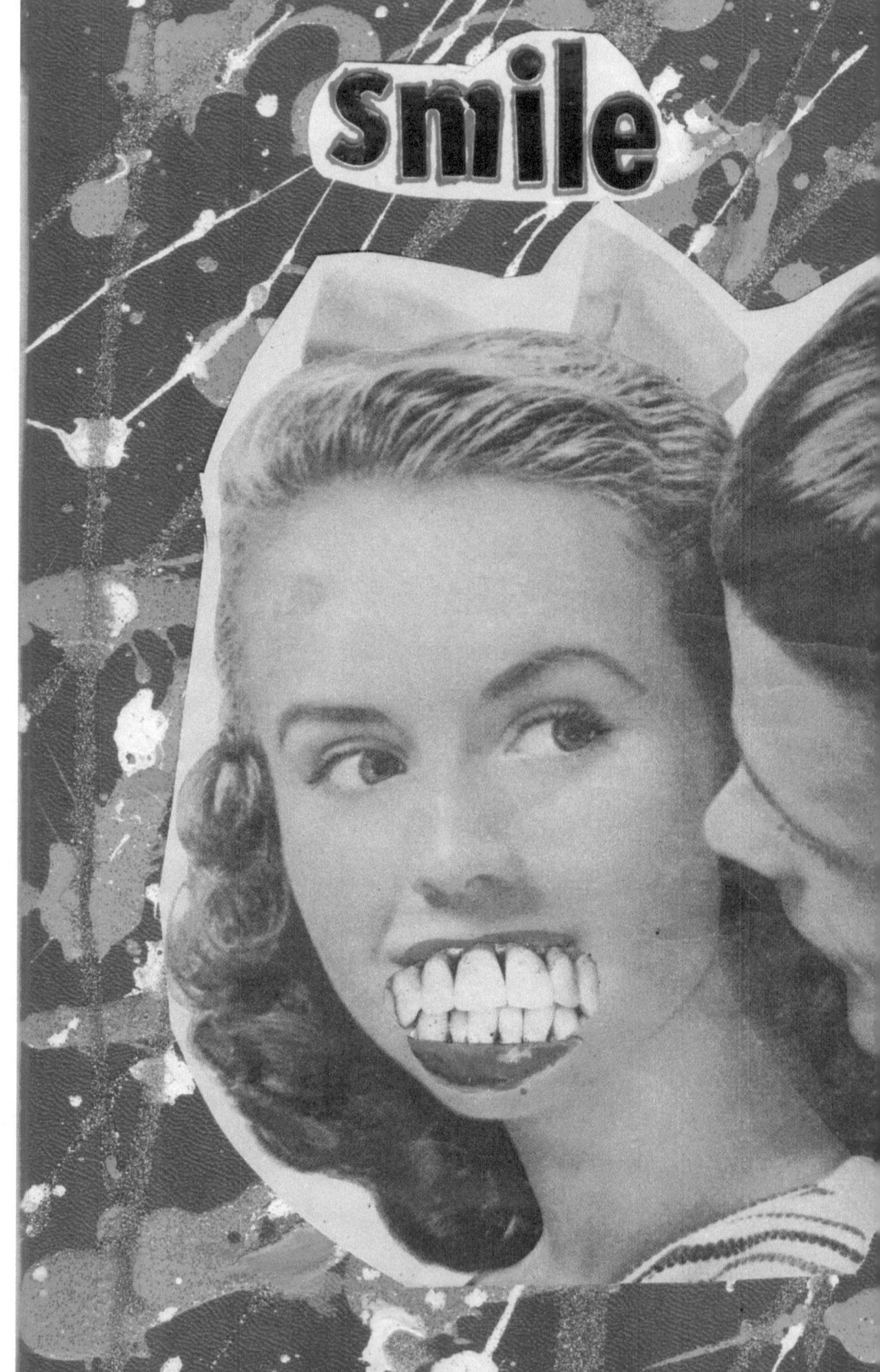

WHEN I SIN
I SIN REAL GOOD

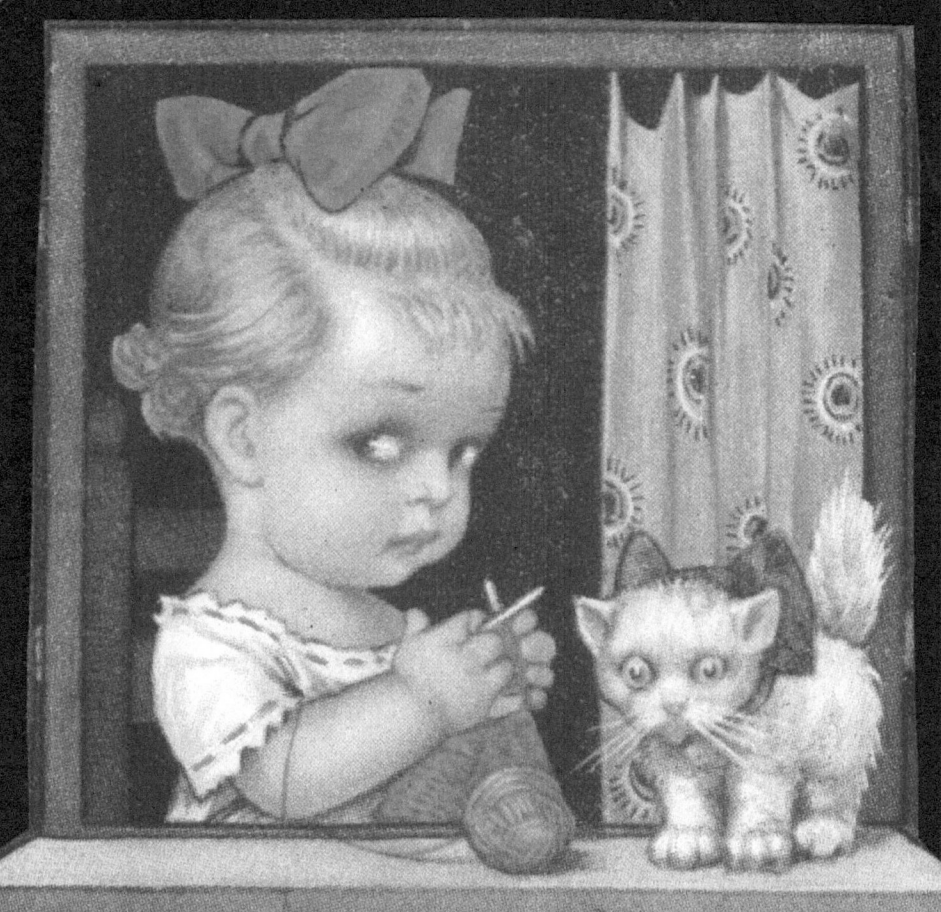

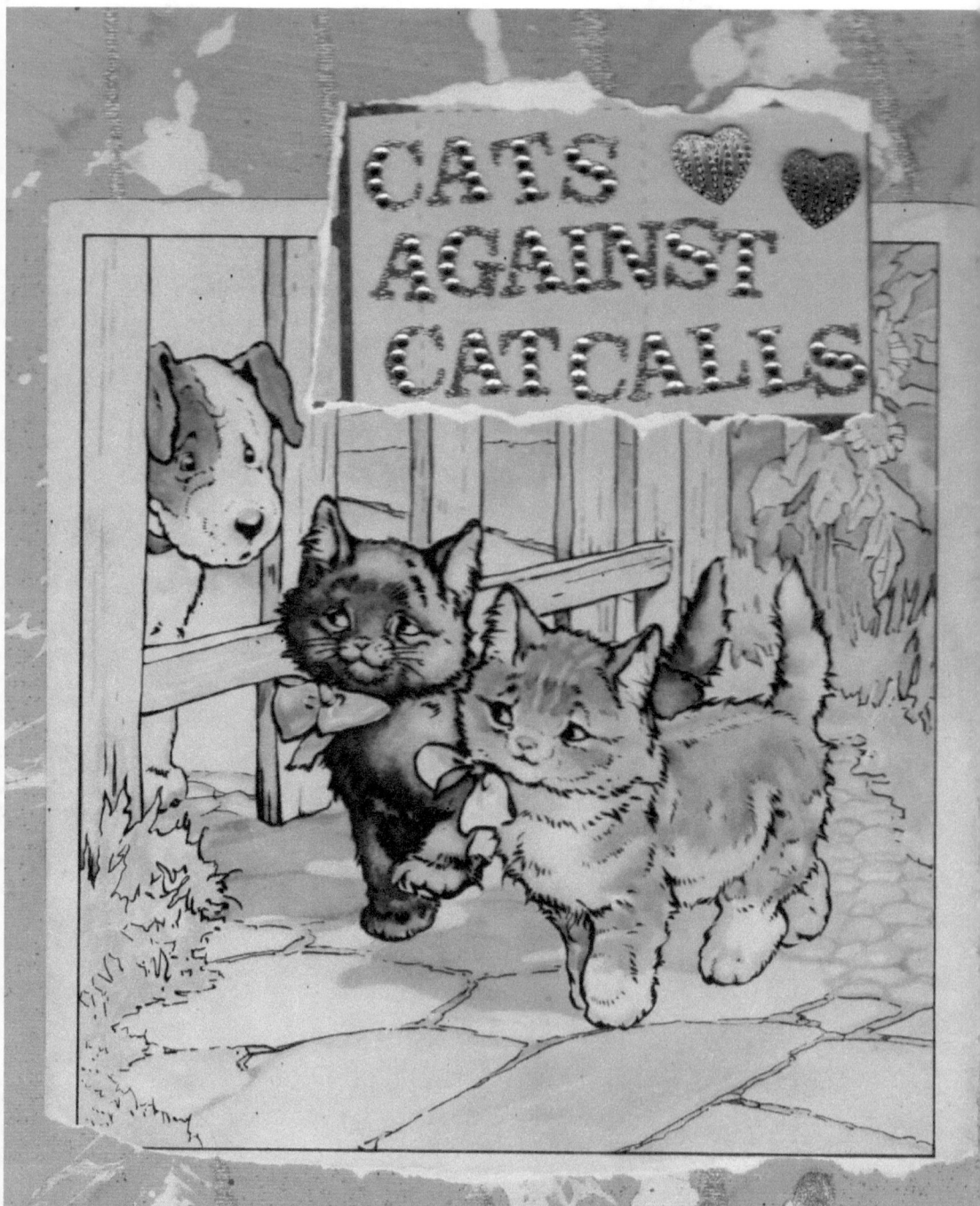

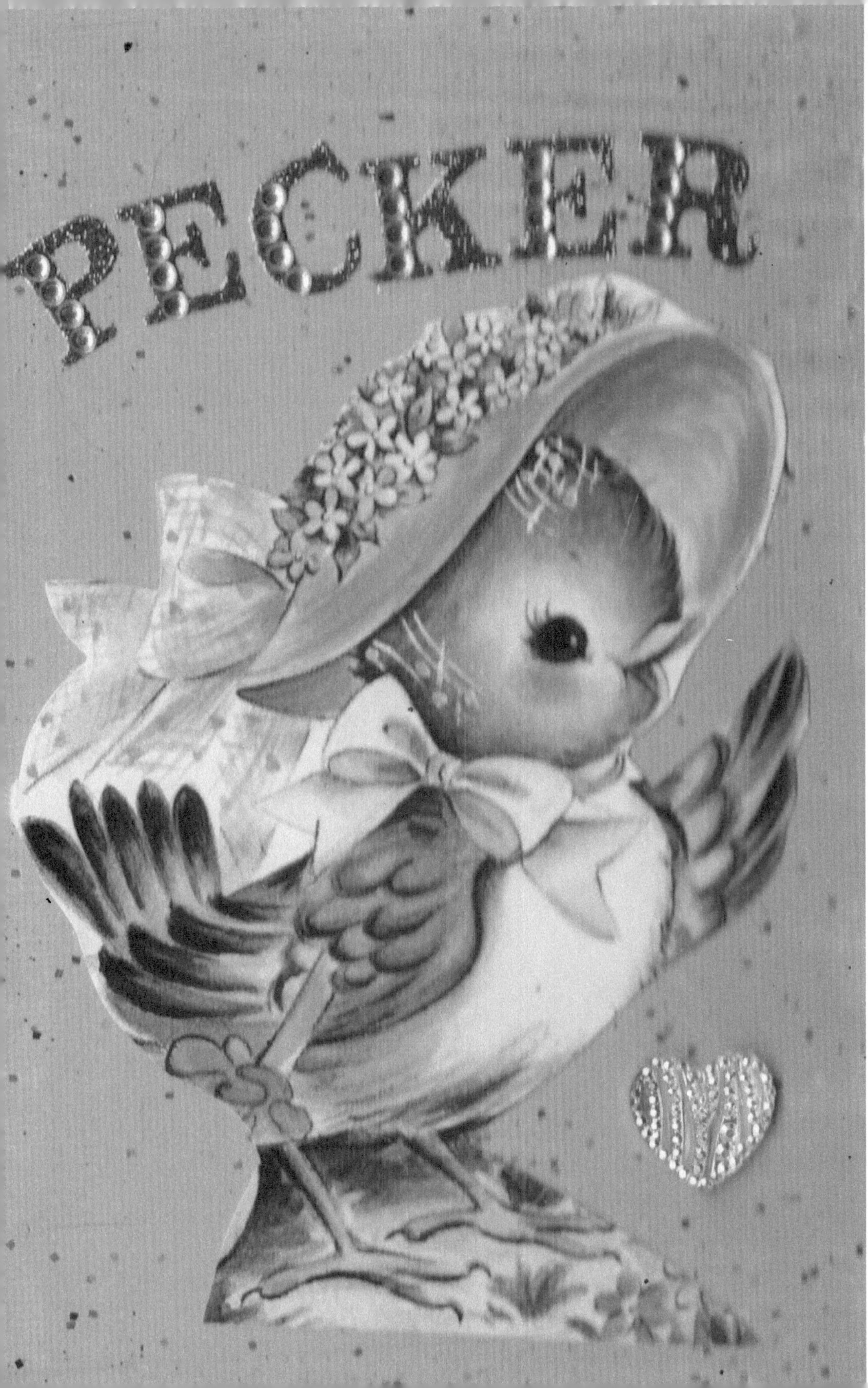
PECKER

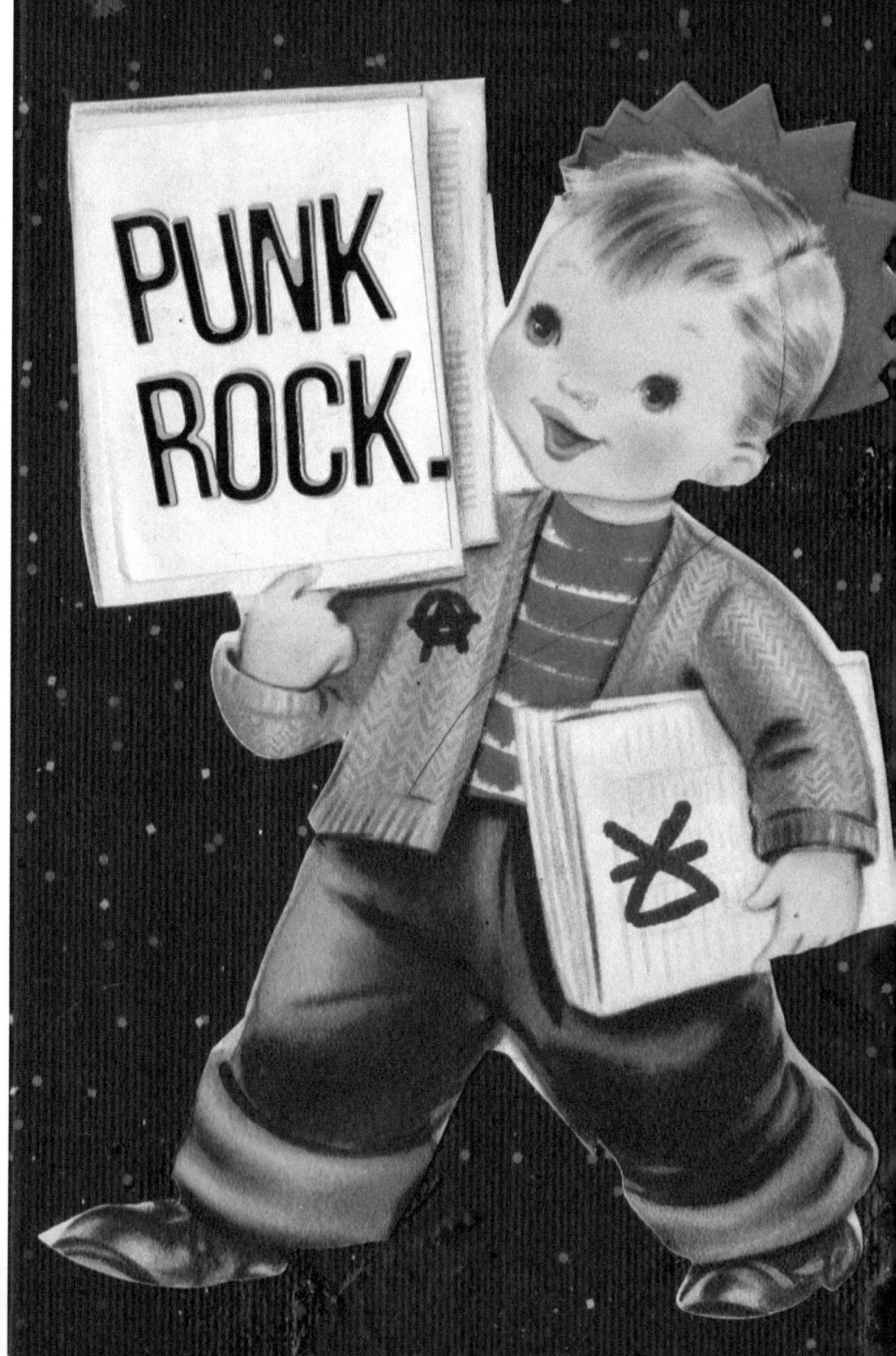

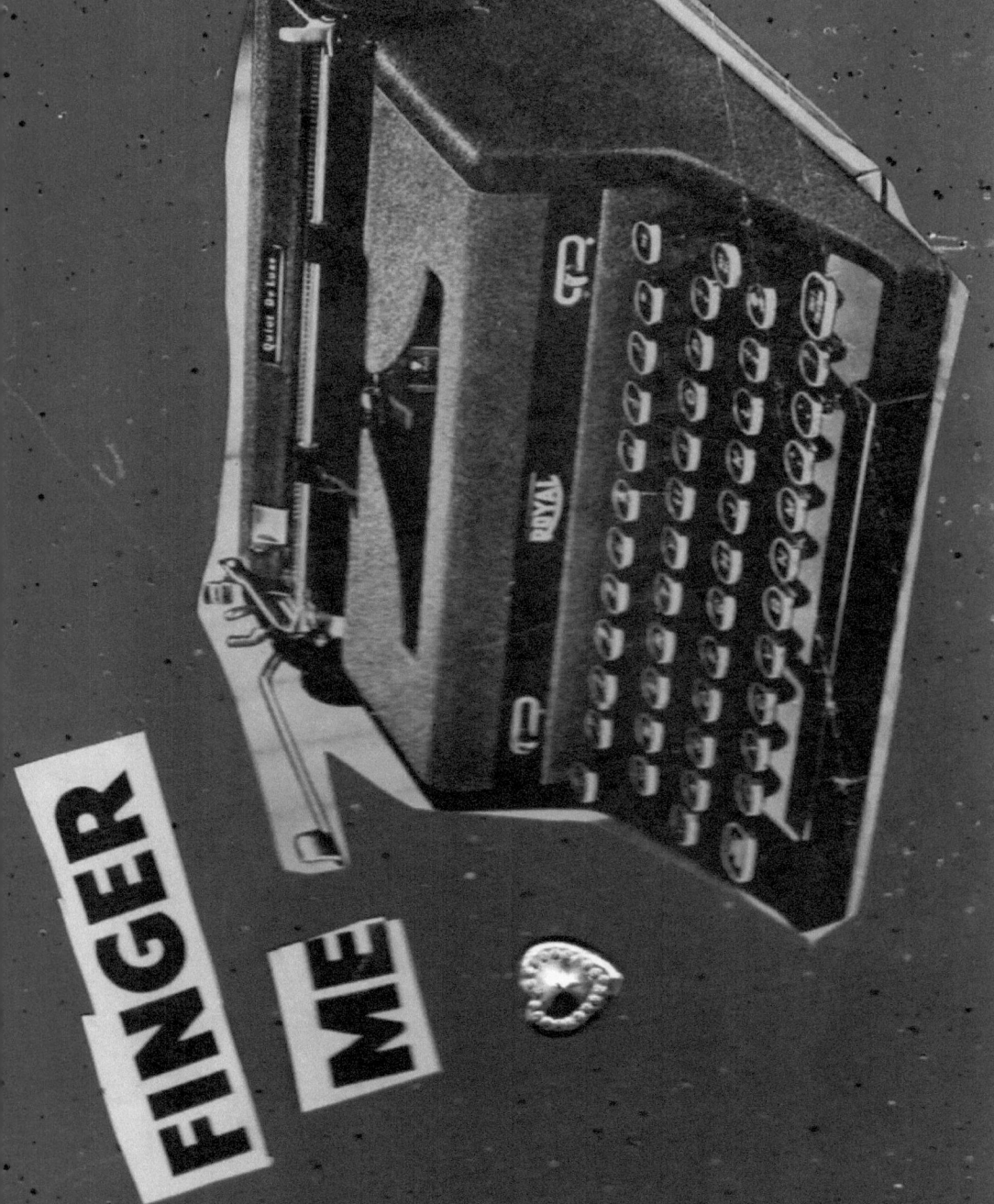

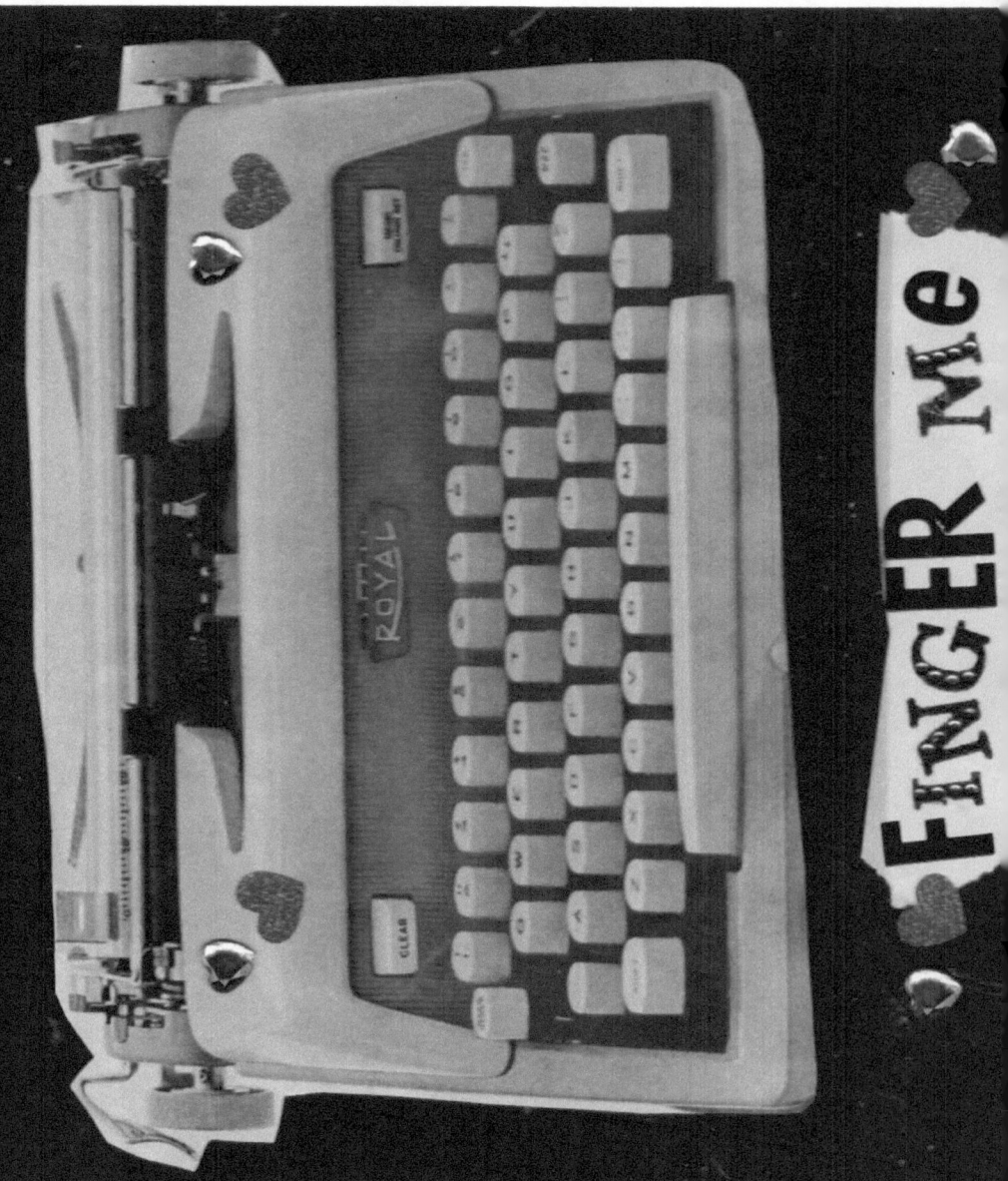

manipulate me

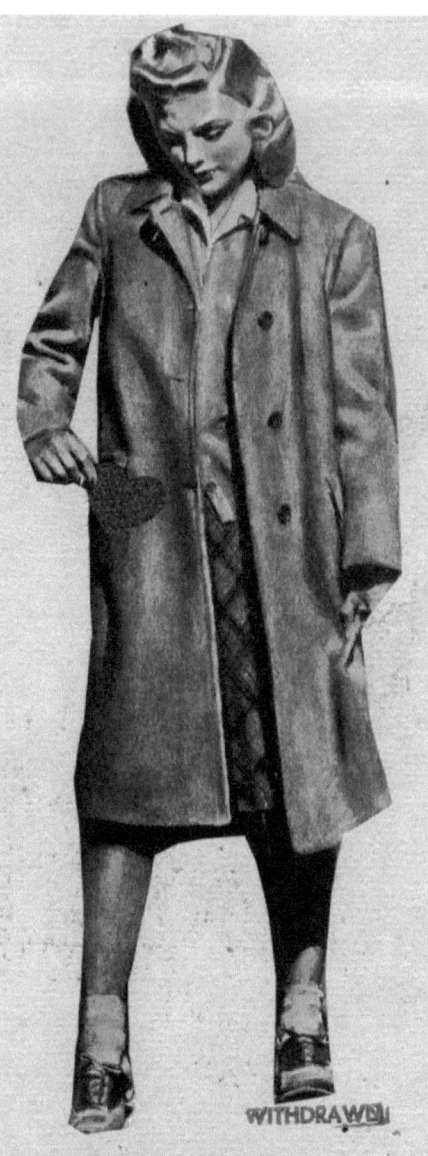

NO FRIENDS

1 LIKE

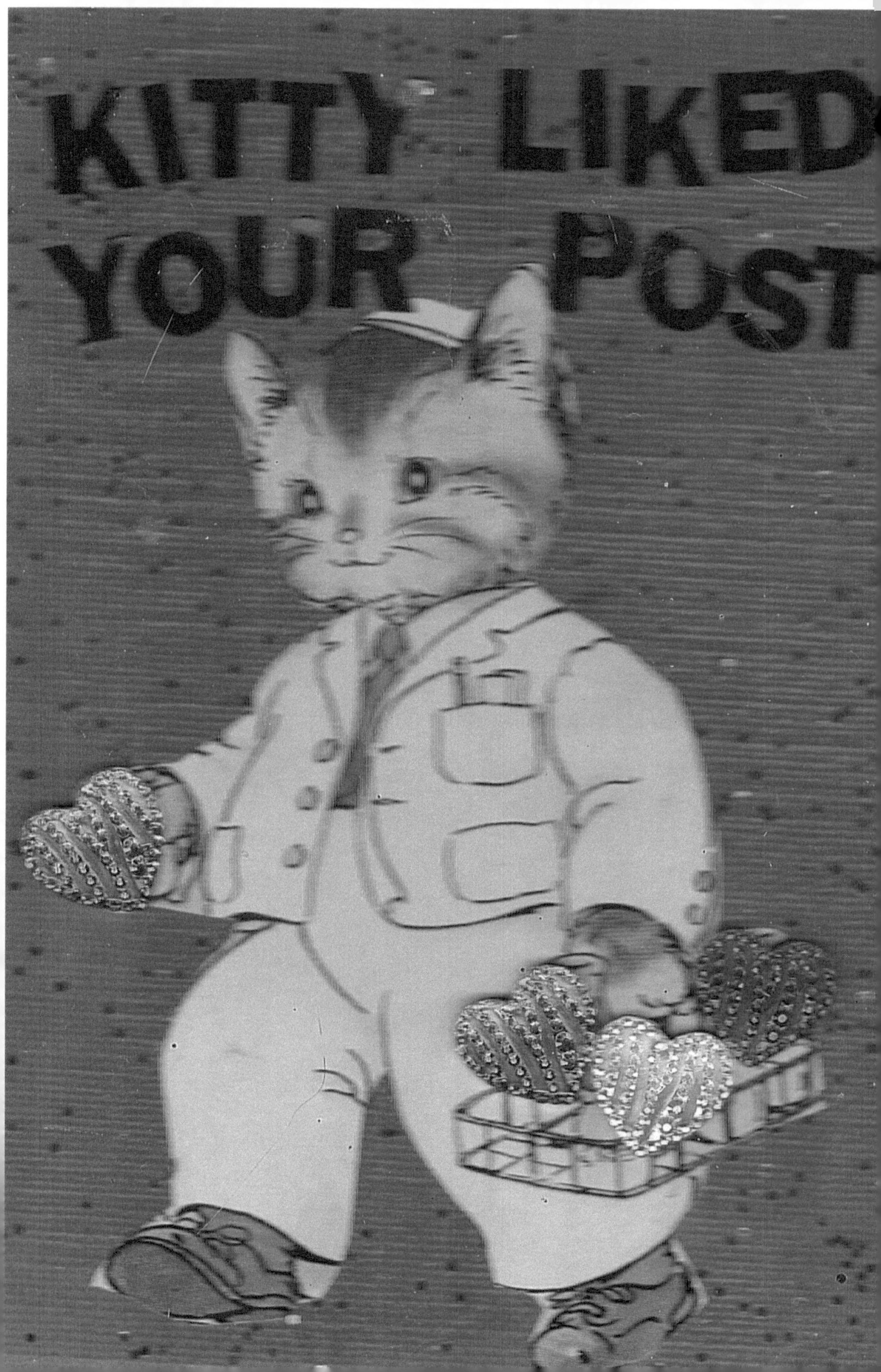
KITTY LIKED
YOUR POST

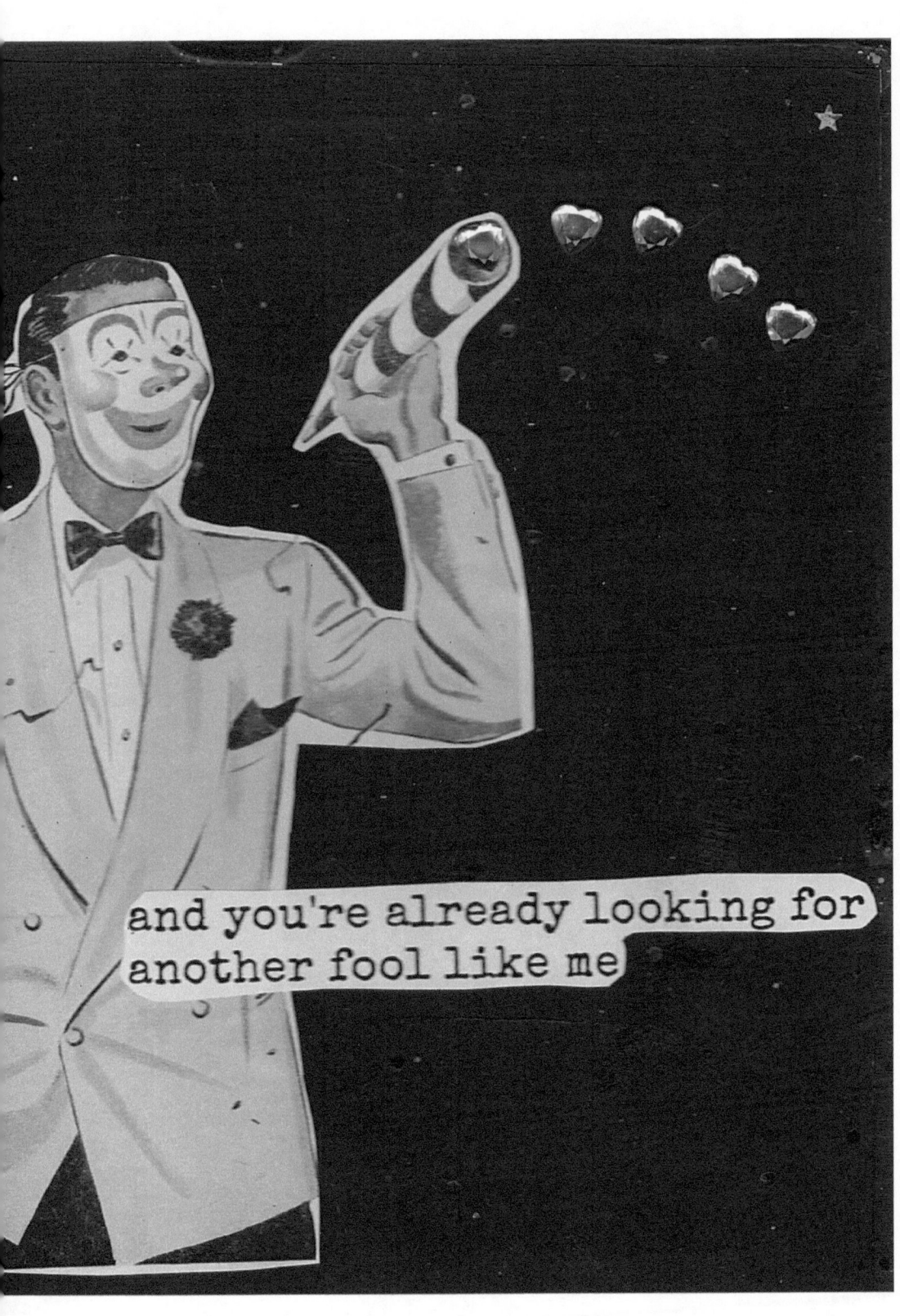

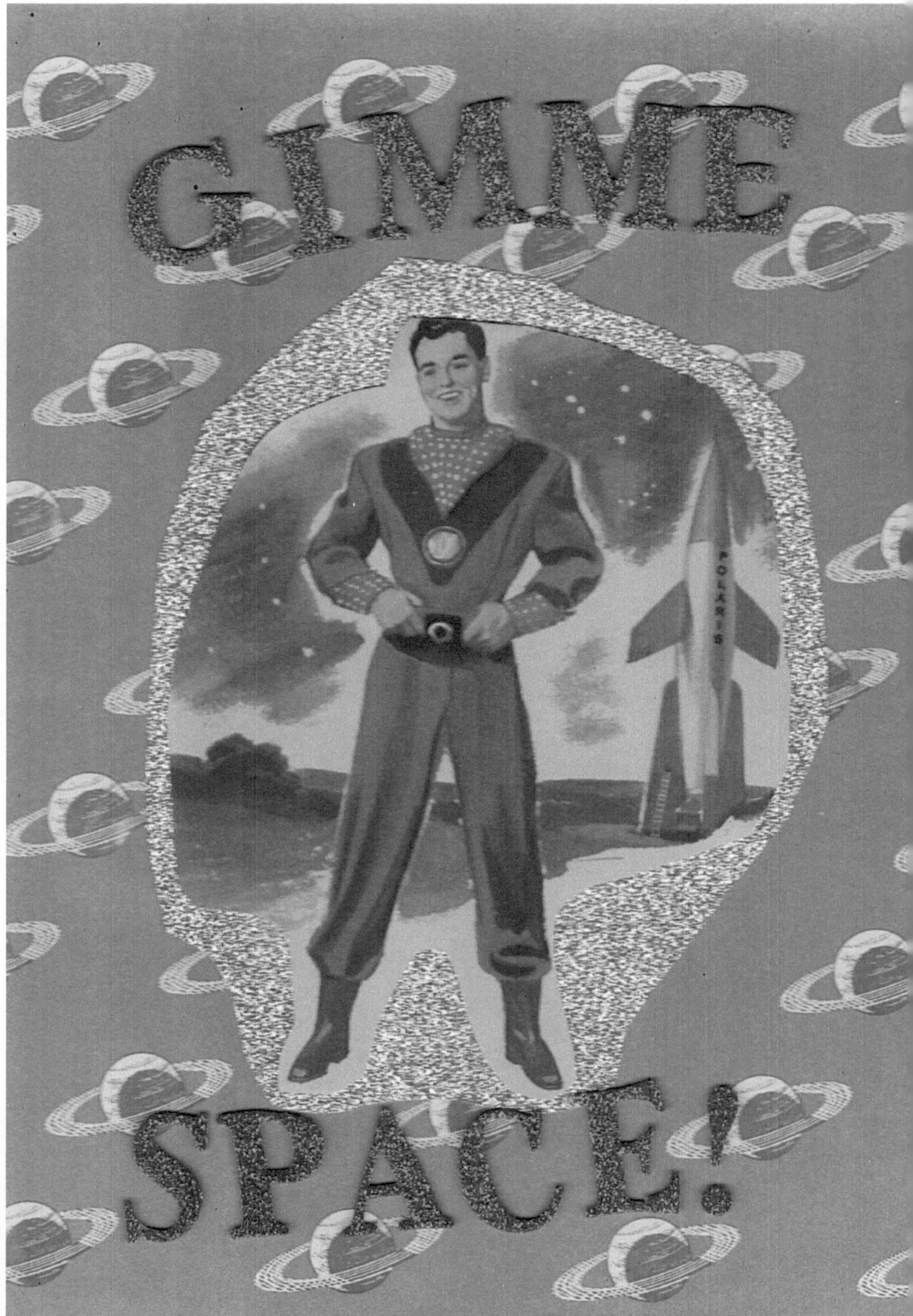

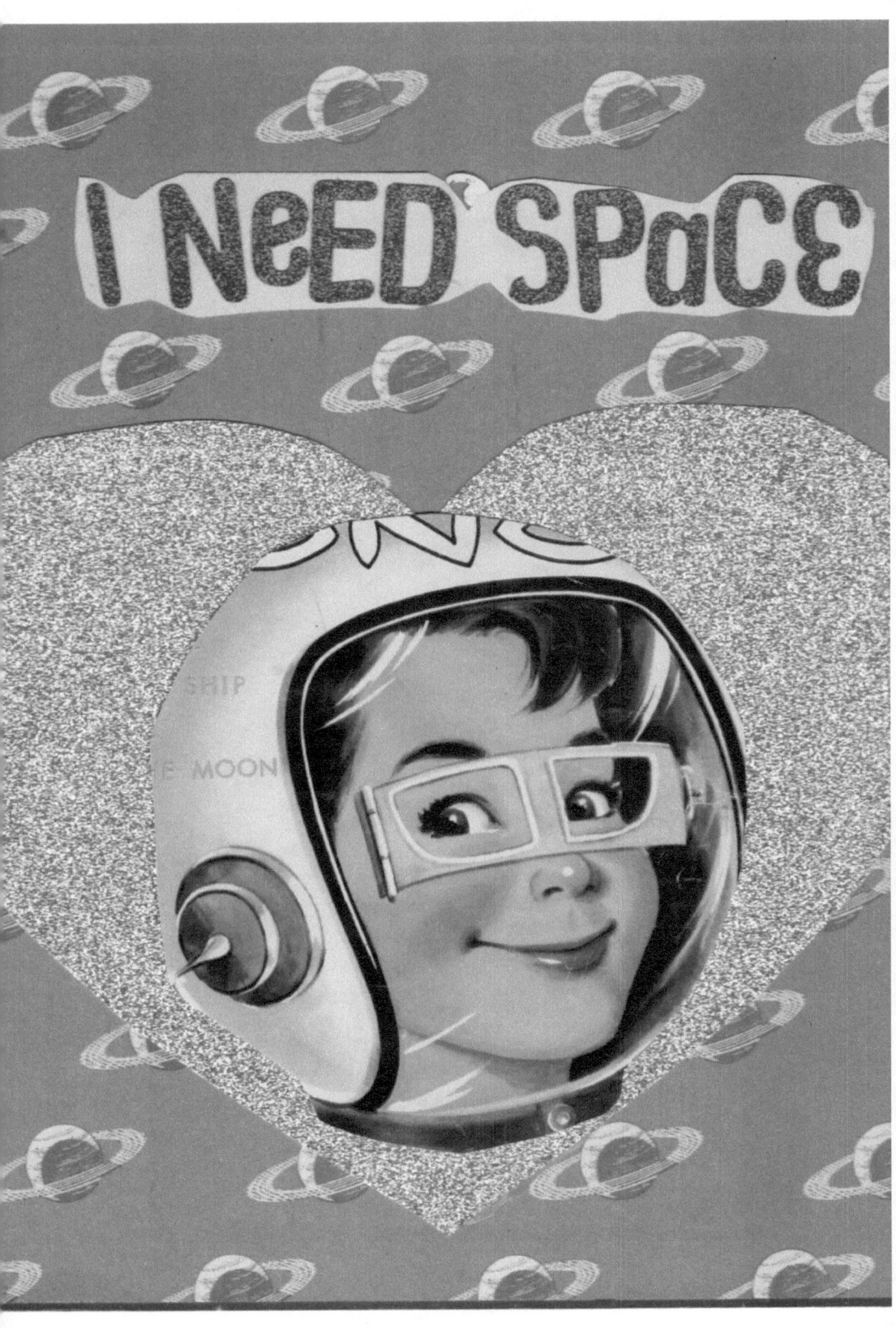

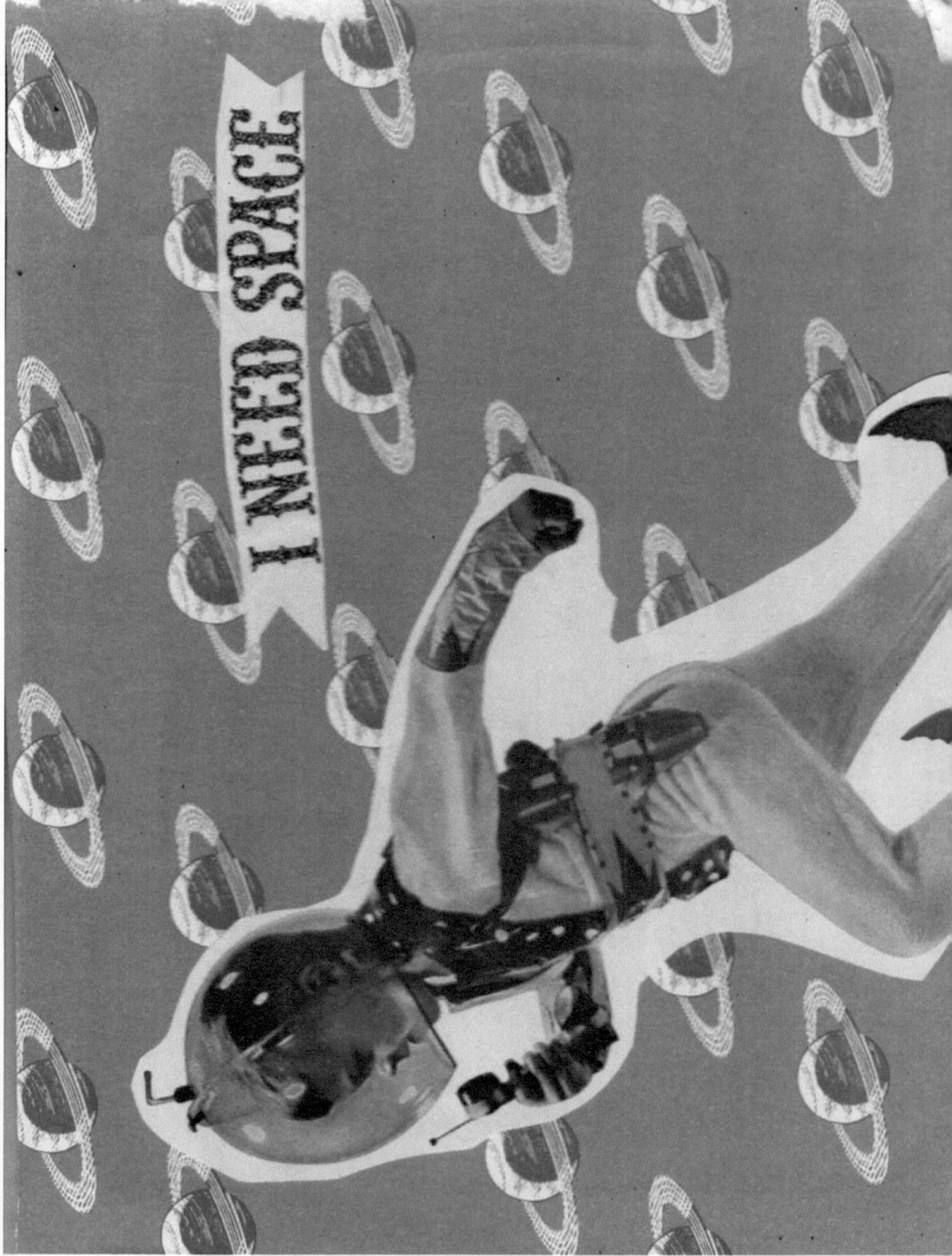

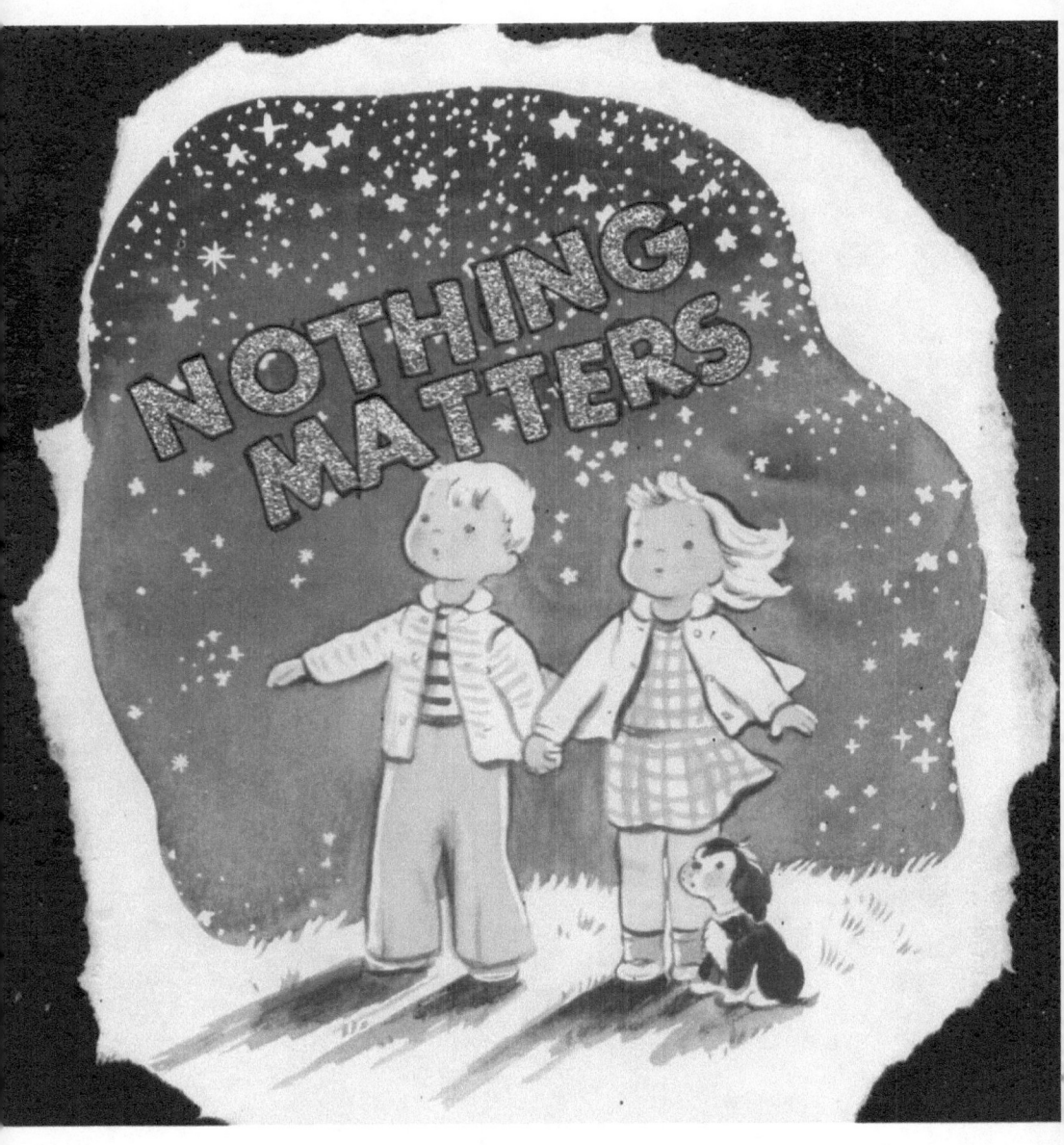

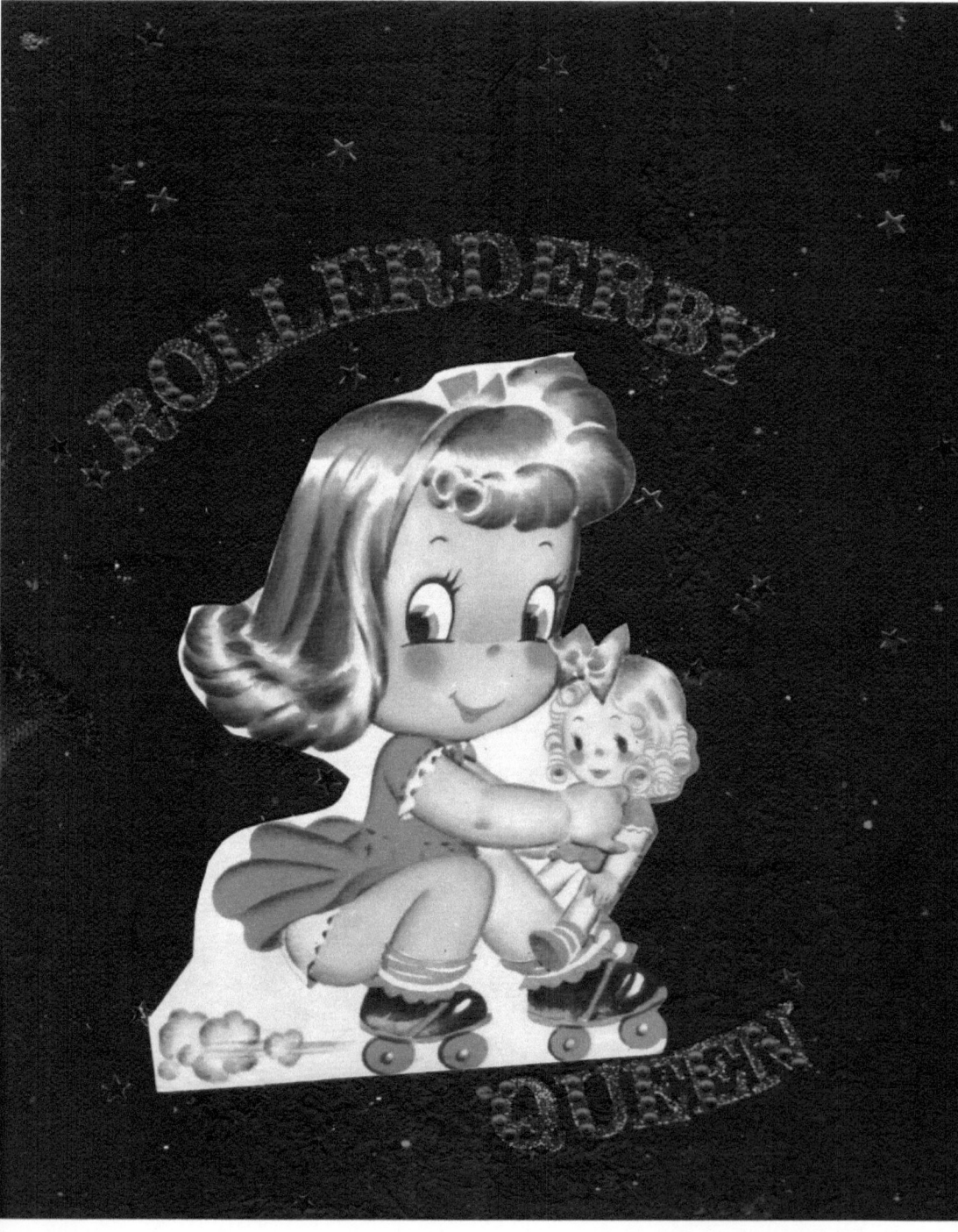

DIE DIE DIE MY DARLING

IT REALLY AIN'T ANARCHY IF IT'S OKAY WITH YOUR MOM

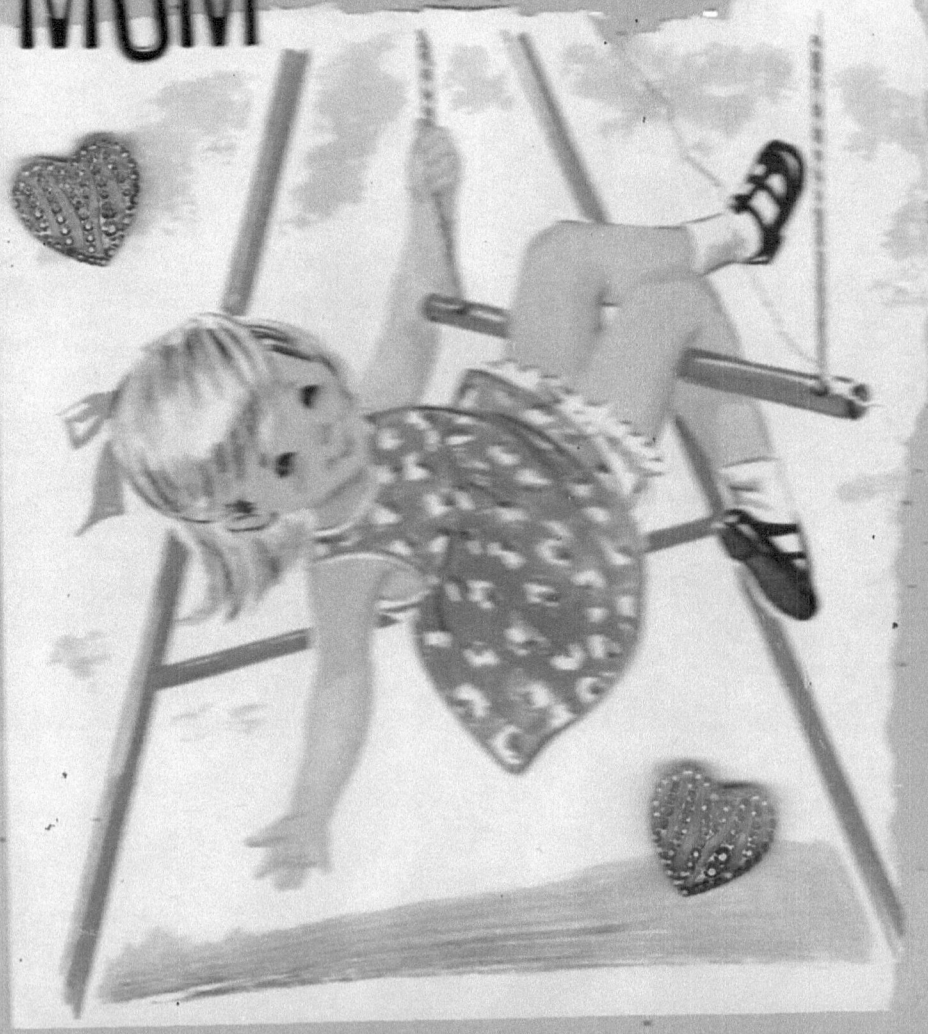

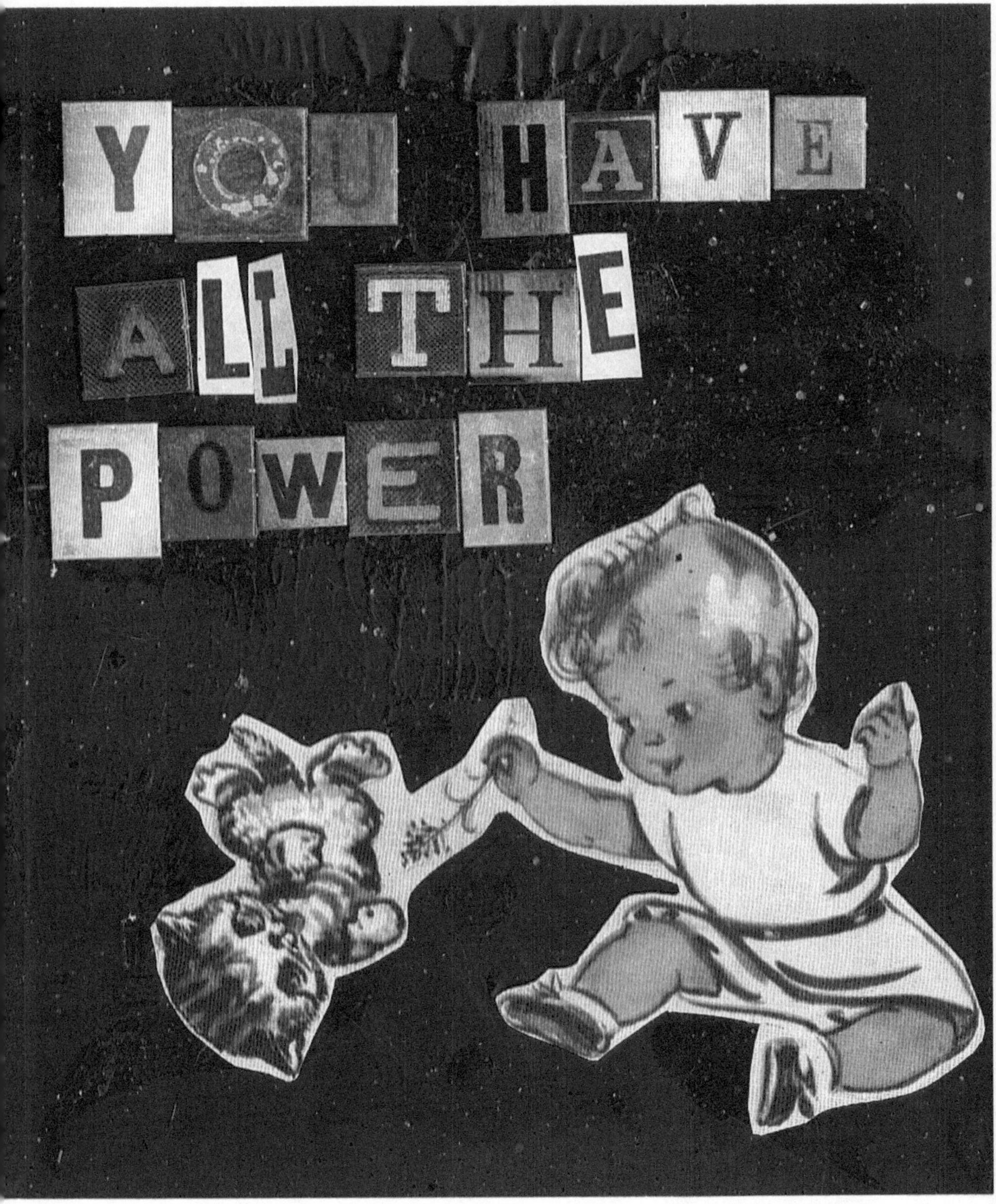
YOU HAVE
ALL THE
POWER

SOMEBODY KILL ME

I'M
MISS
WORLD

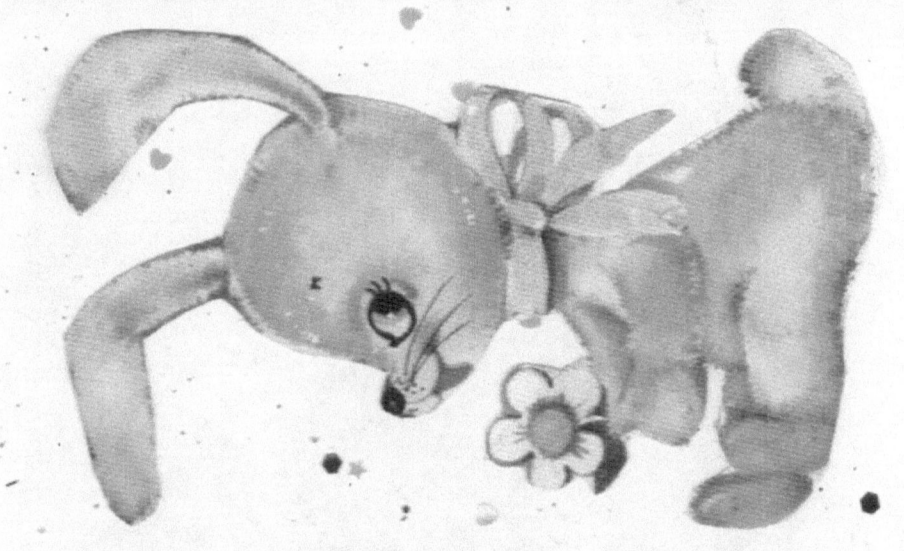

AND I'M THE ONE WITH NO SOUL

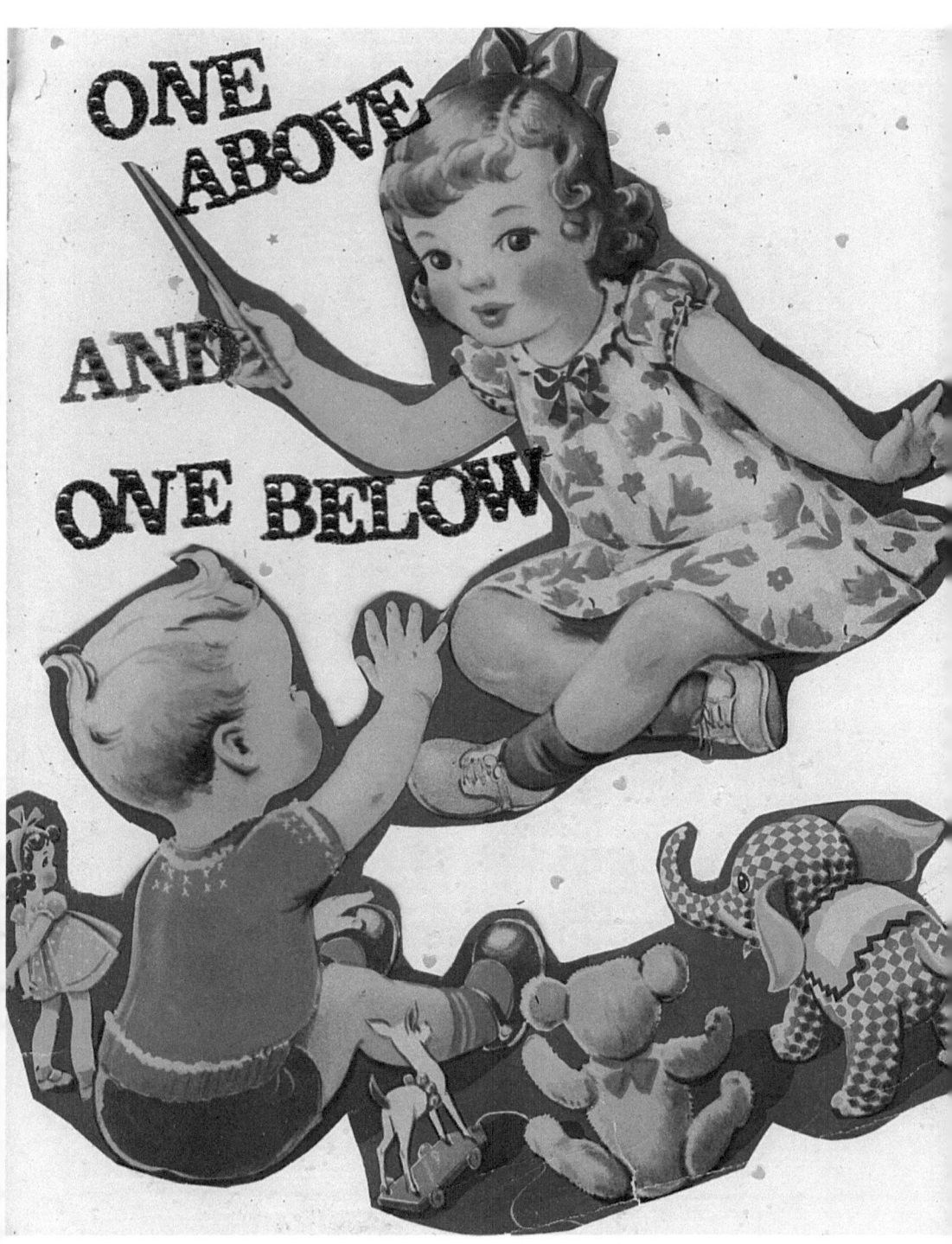

ONE ABOVE
AND
ONE BELOW

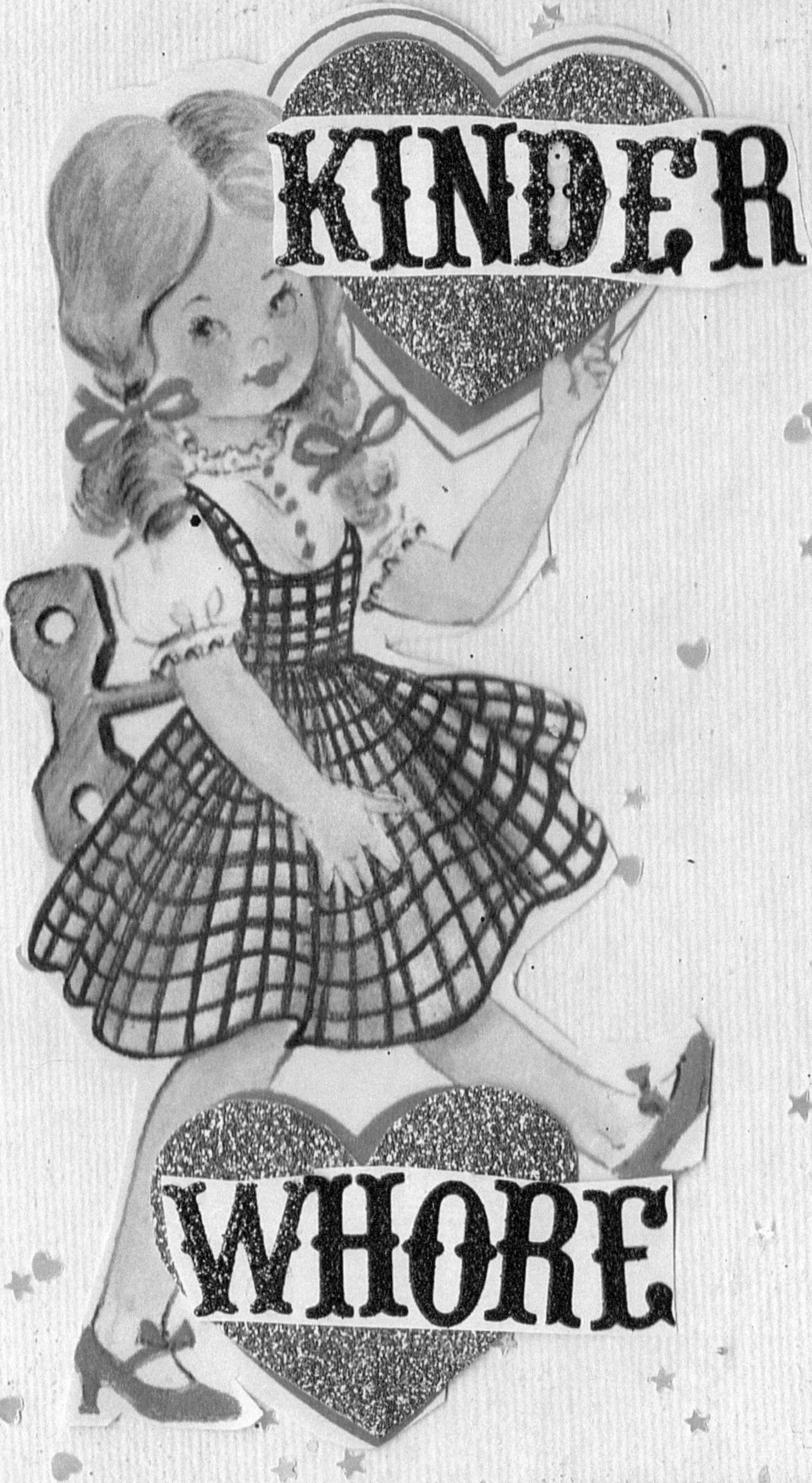
KINDER
WHORE

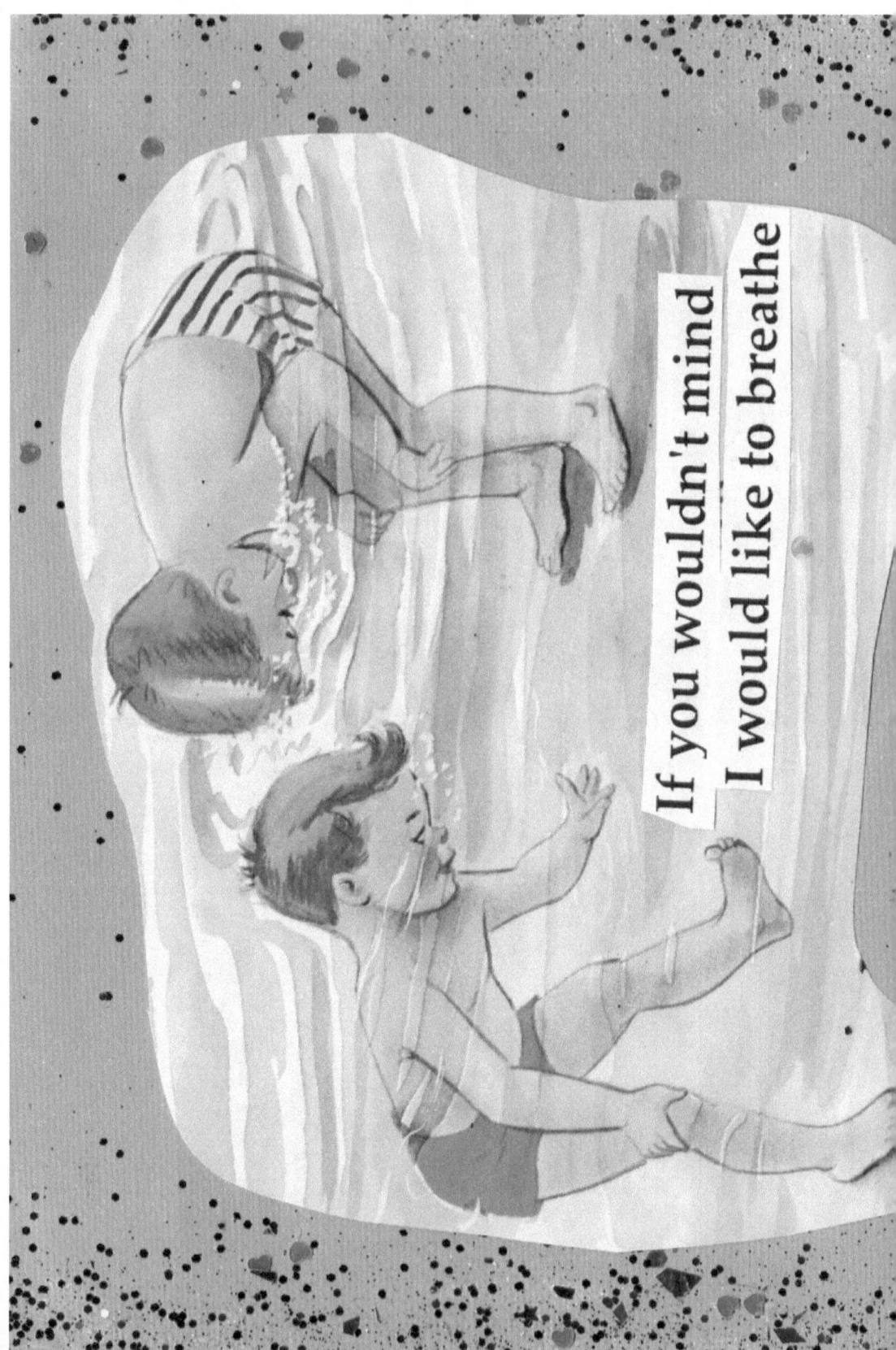

If you wouldn't mind
I would like to breathe

AND I'M TIRED OF BEING ALIVE

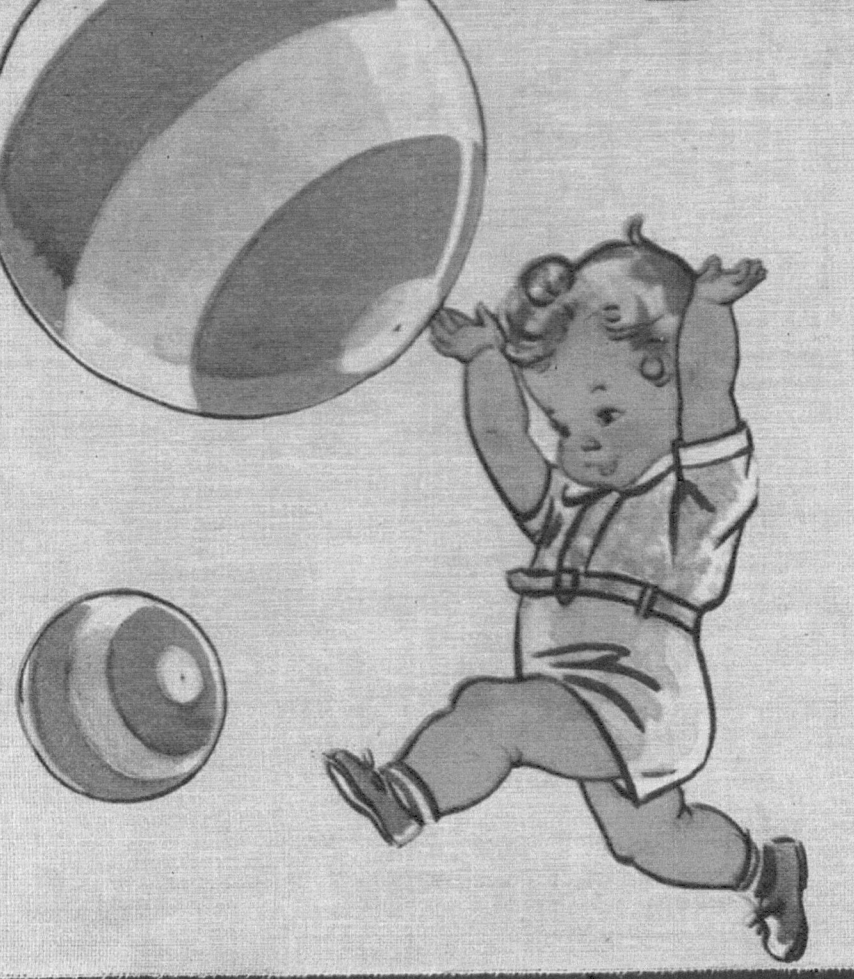

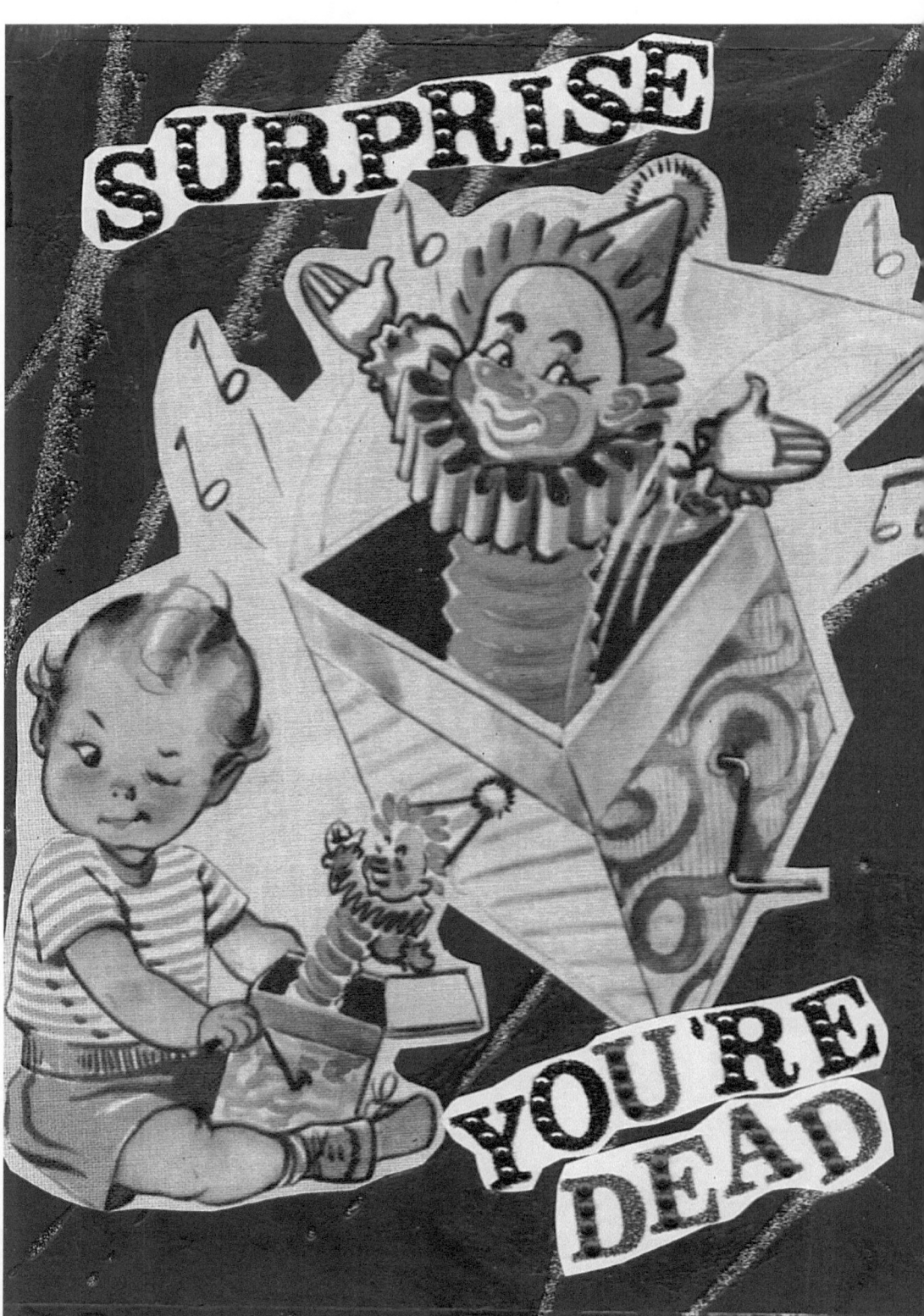

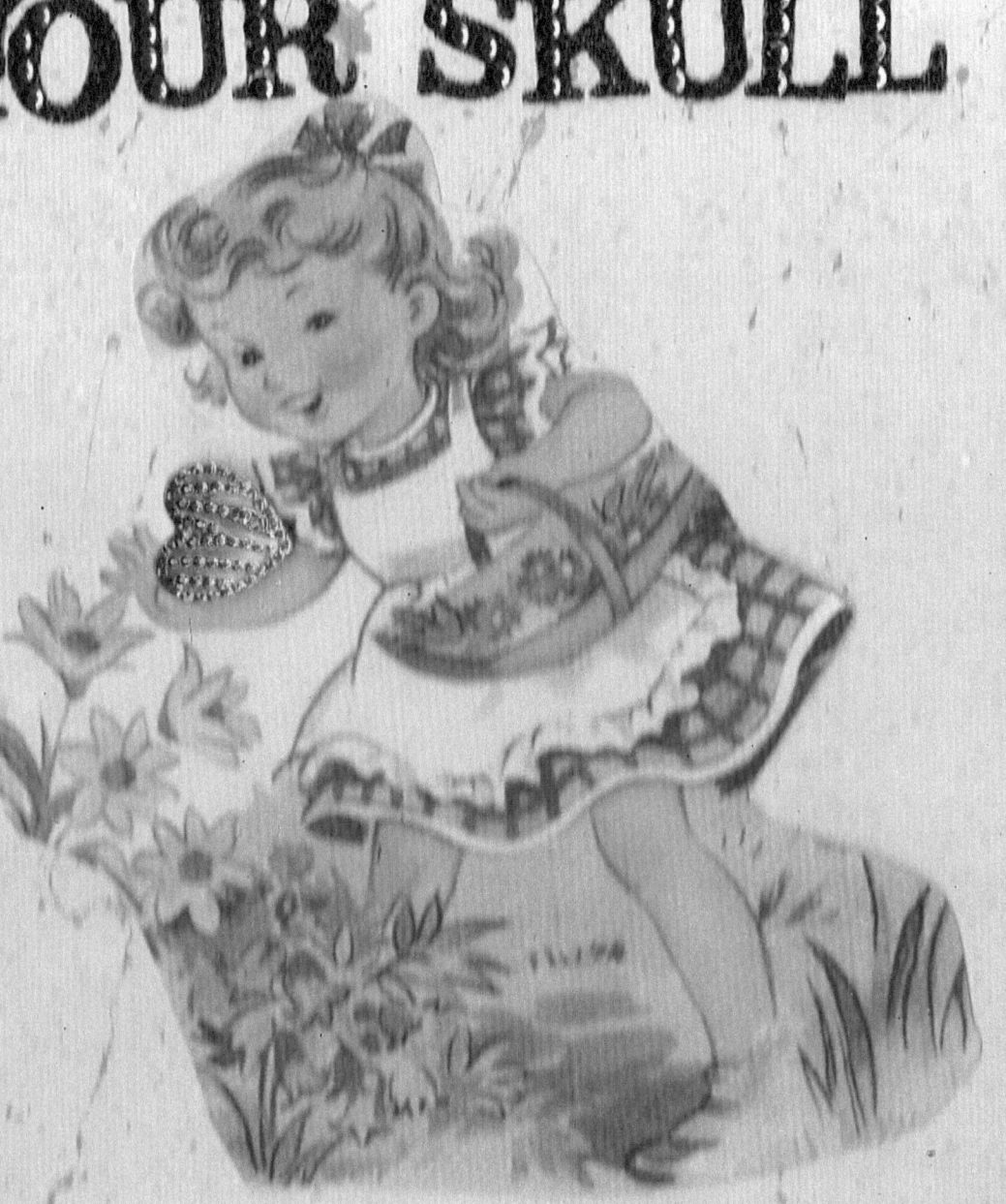

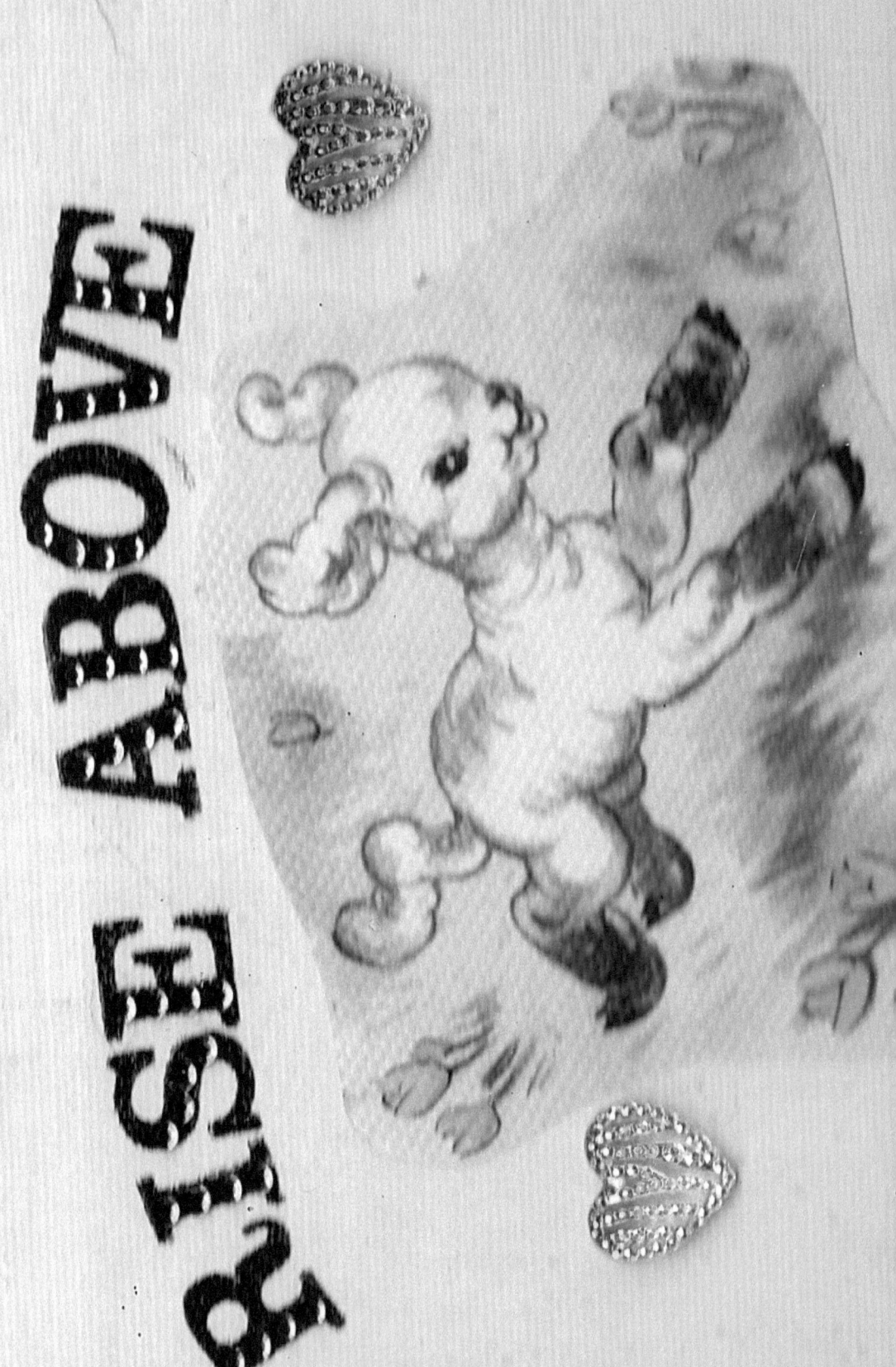

EAT YOUR FEELINGS

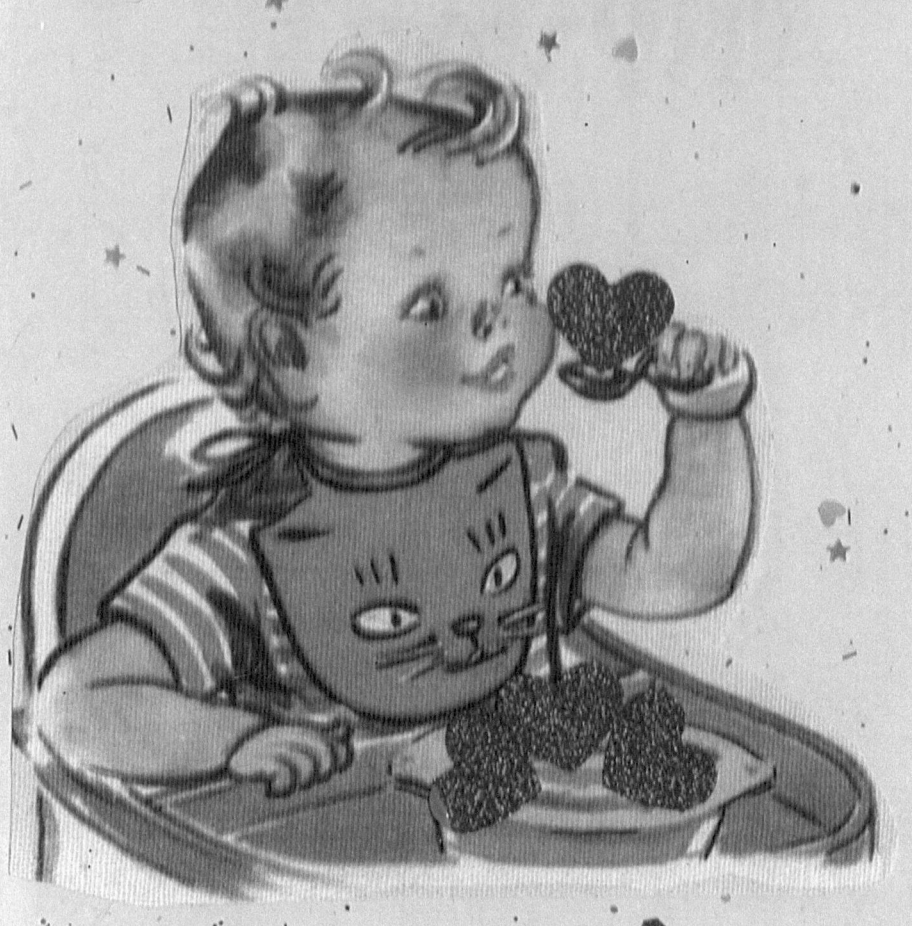

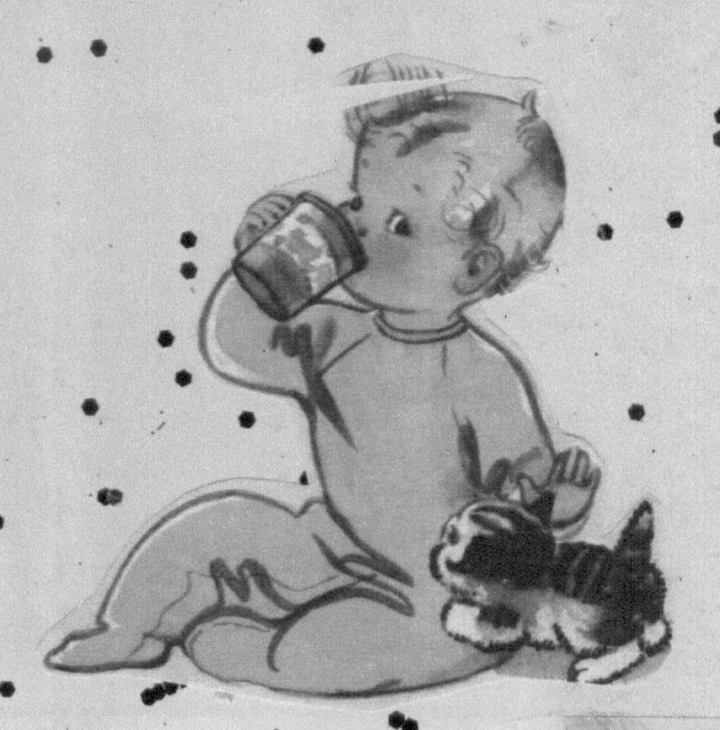

YOU ARE ANNOYING

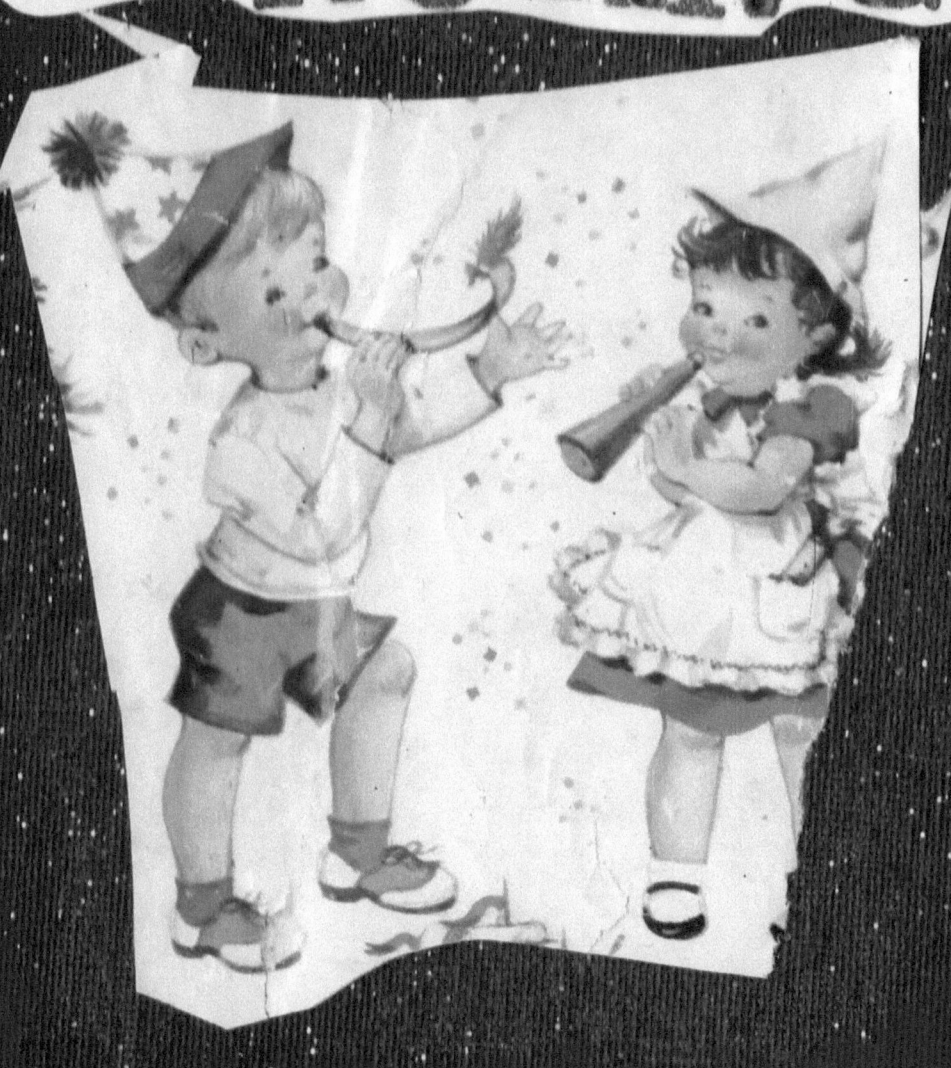

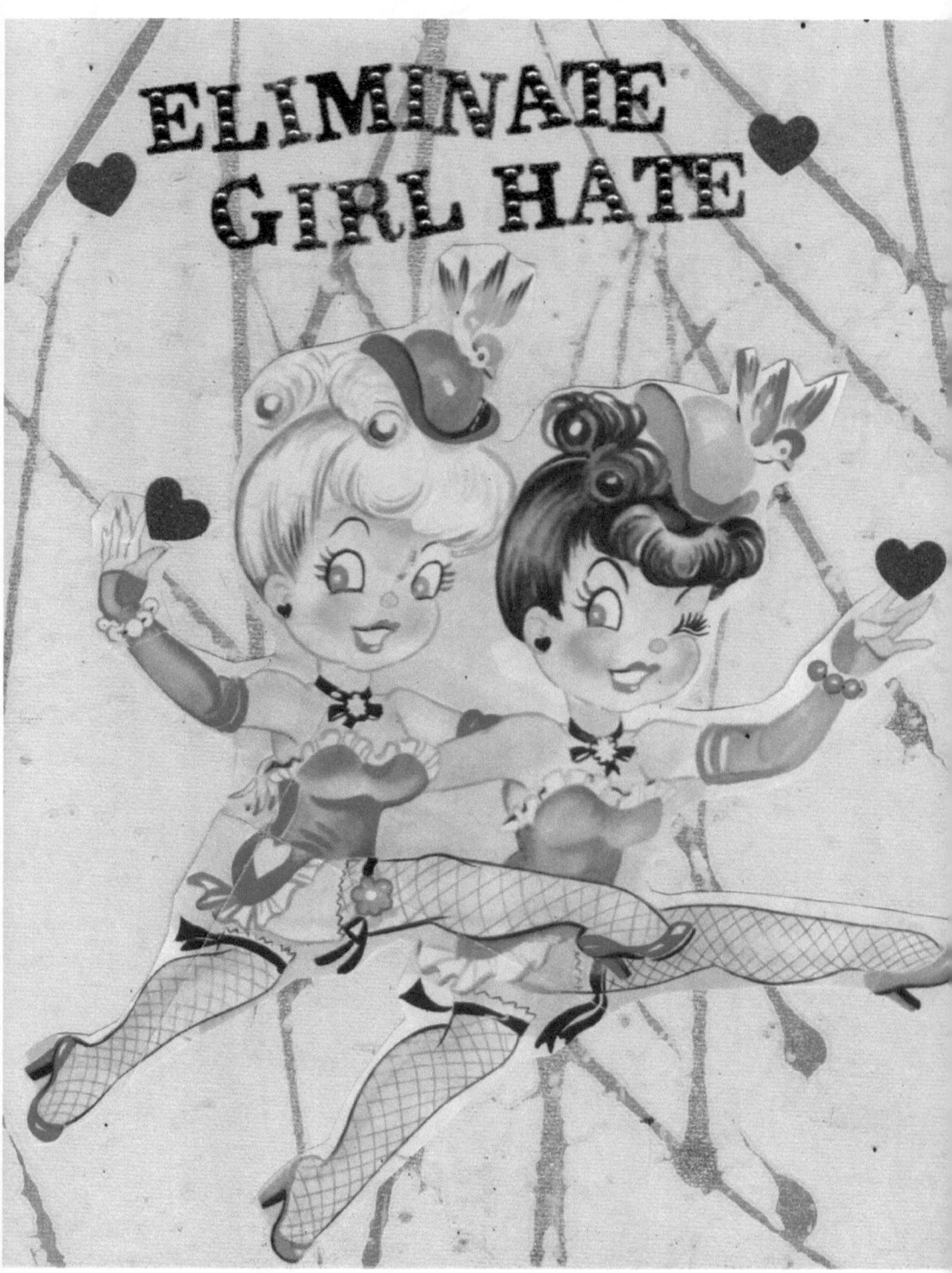

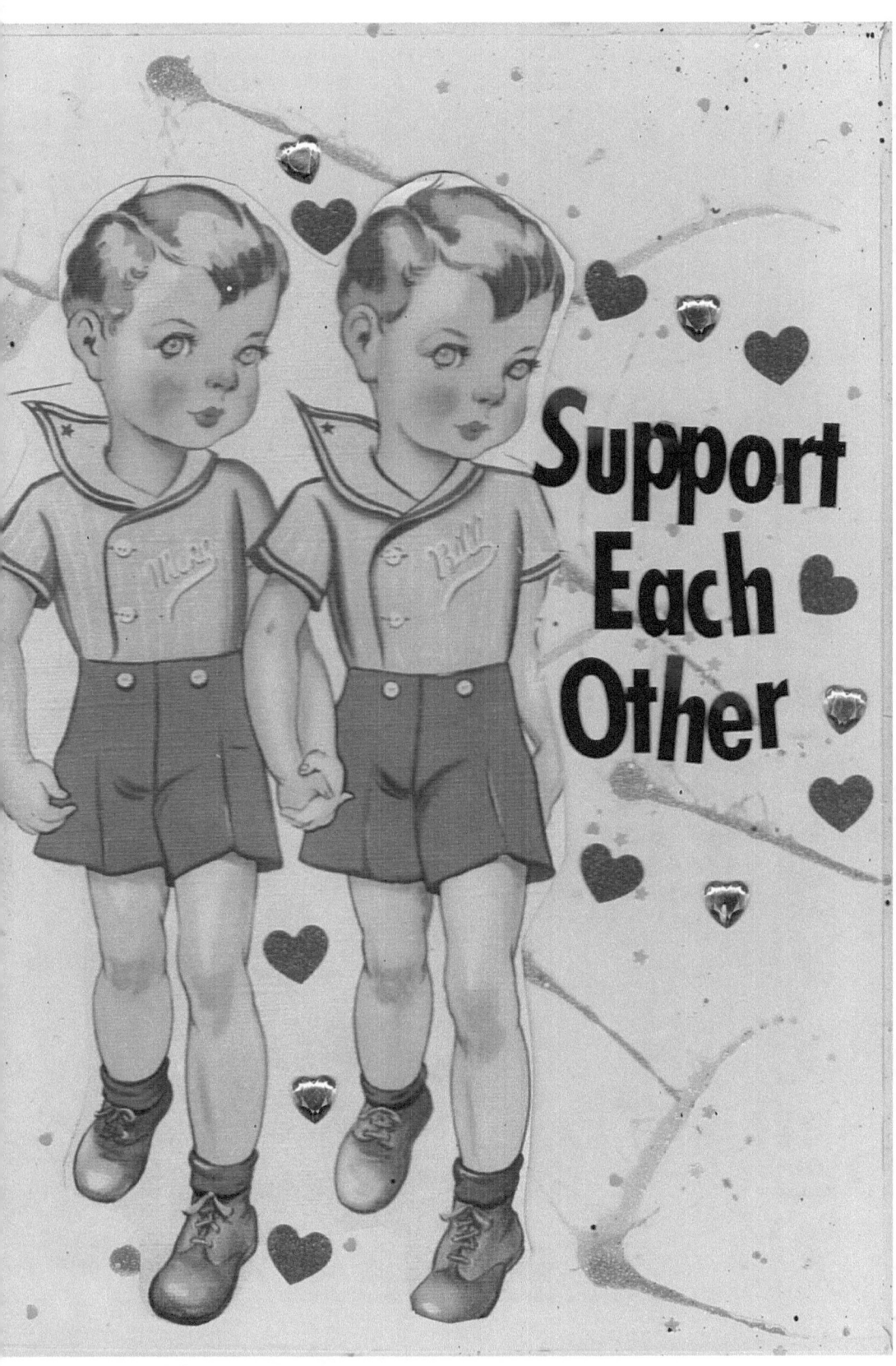

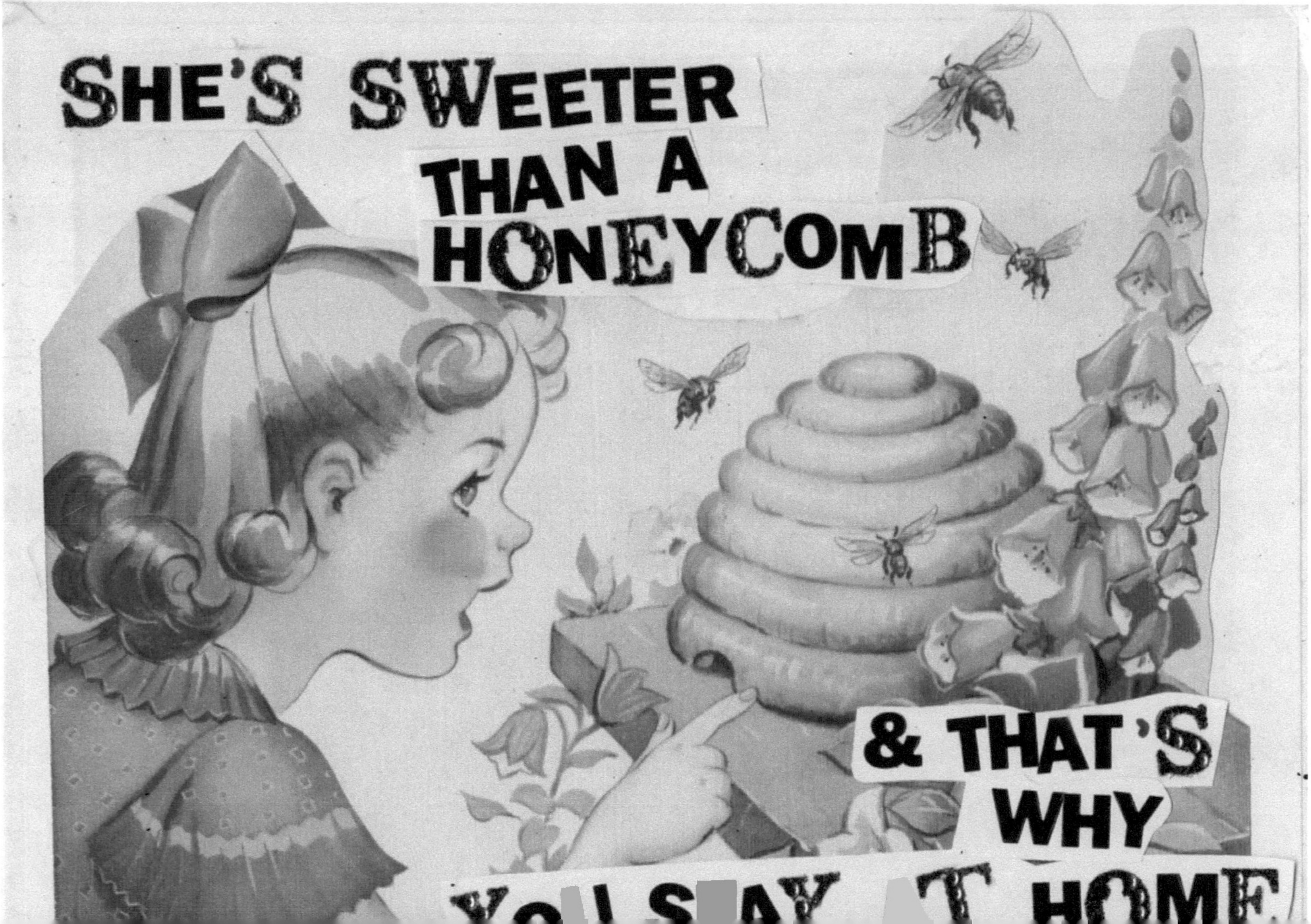
SHE'S SWEETER
THAN A
HONEYCOMB
& THAT'S
WHY

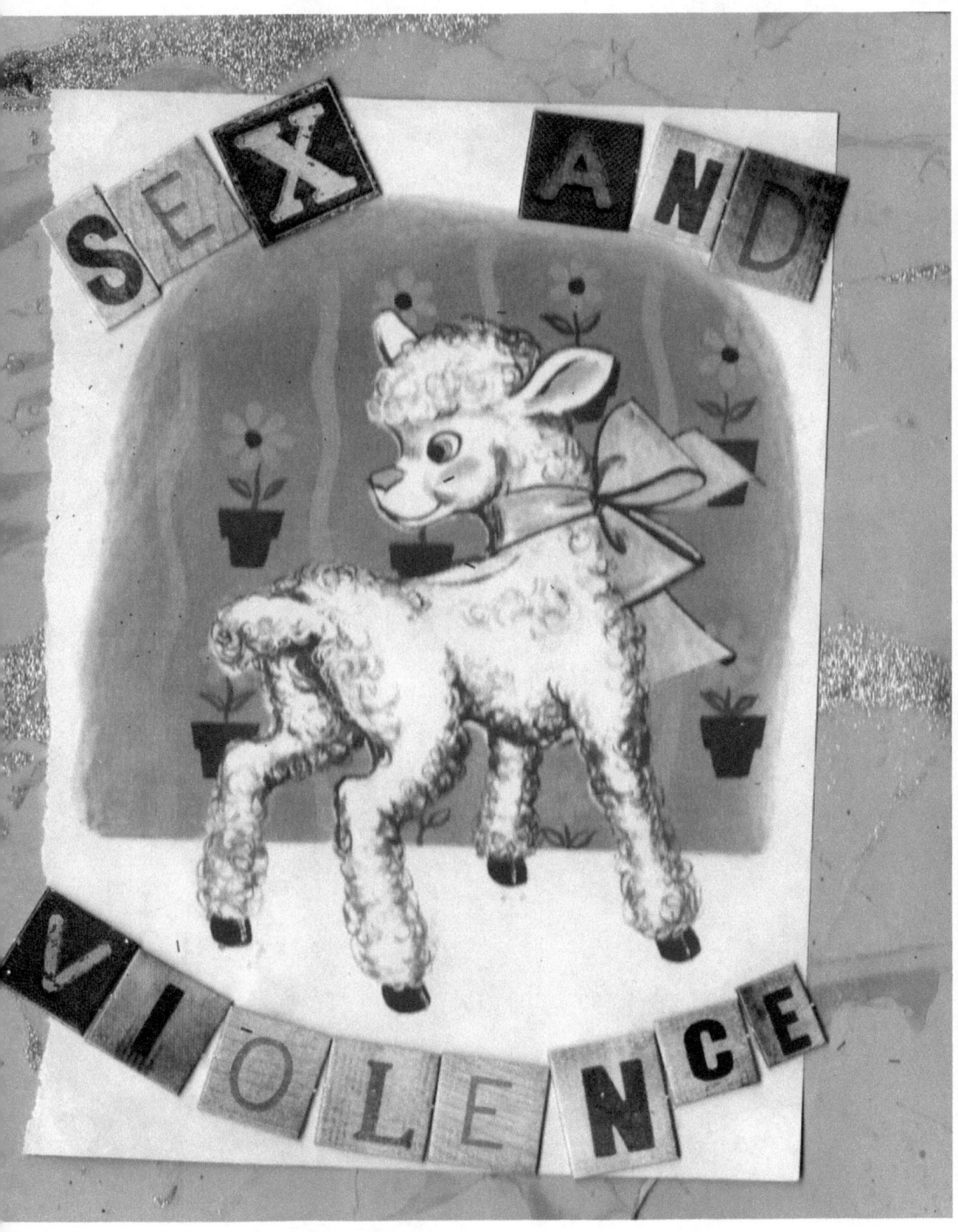

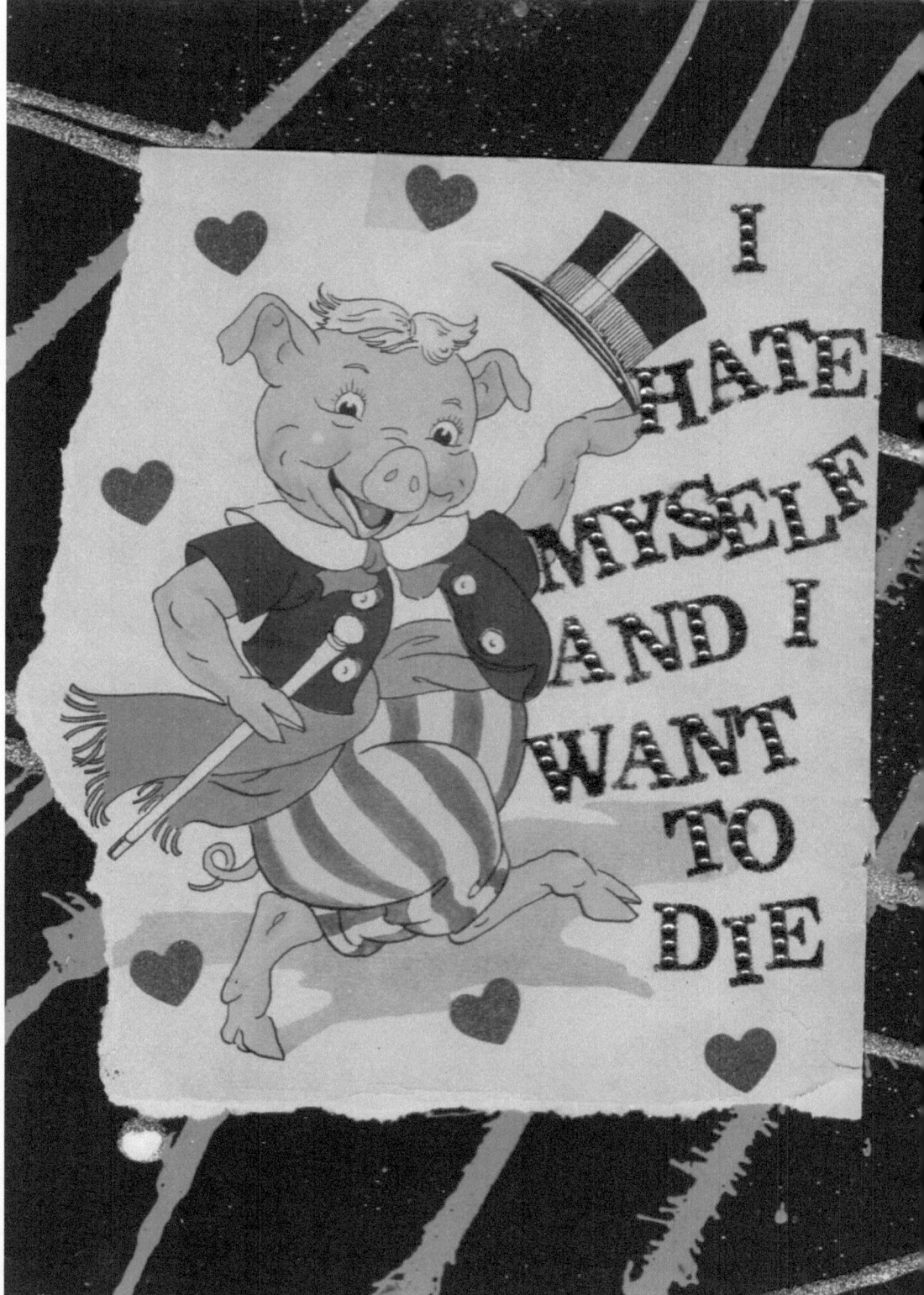

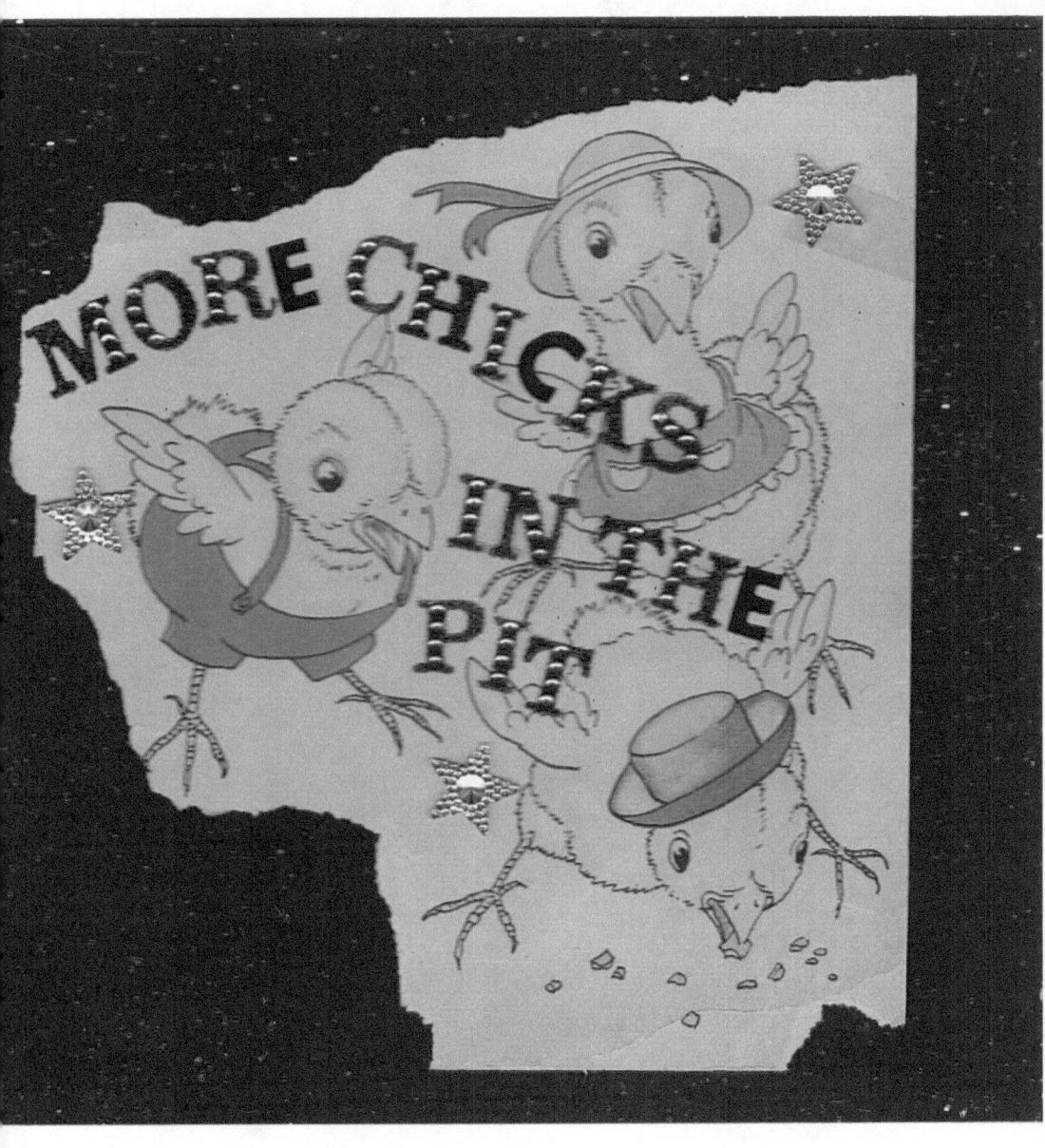

MORE CHICKS IN THE PIT

BRUISE VIOLEt

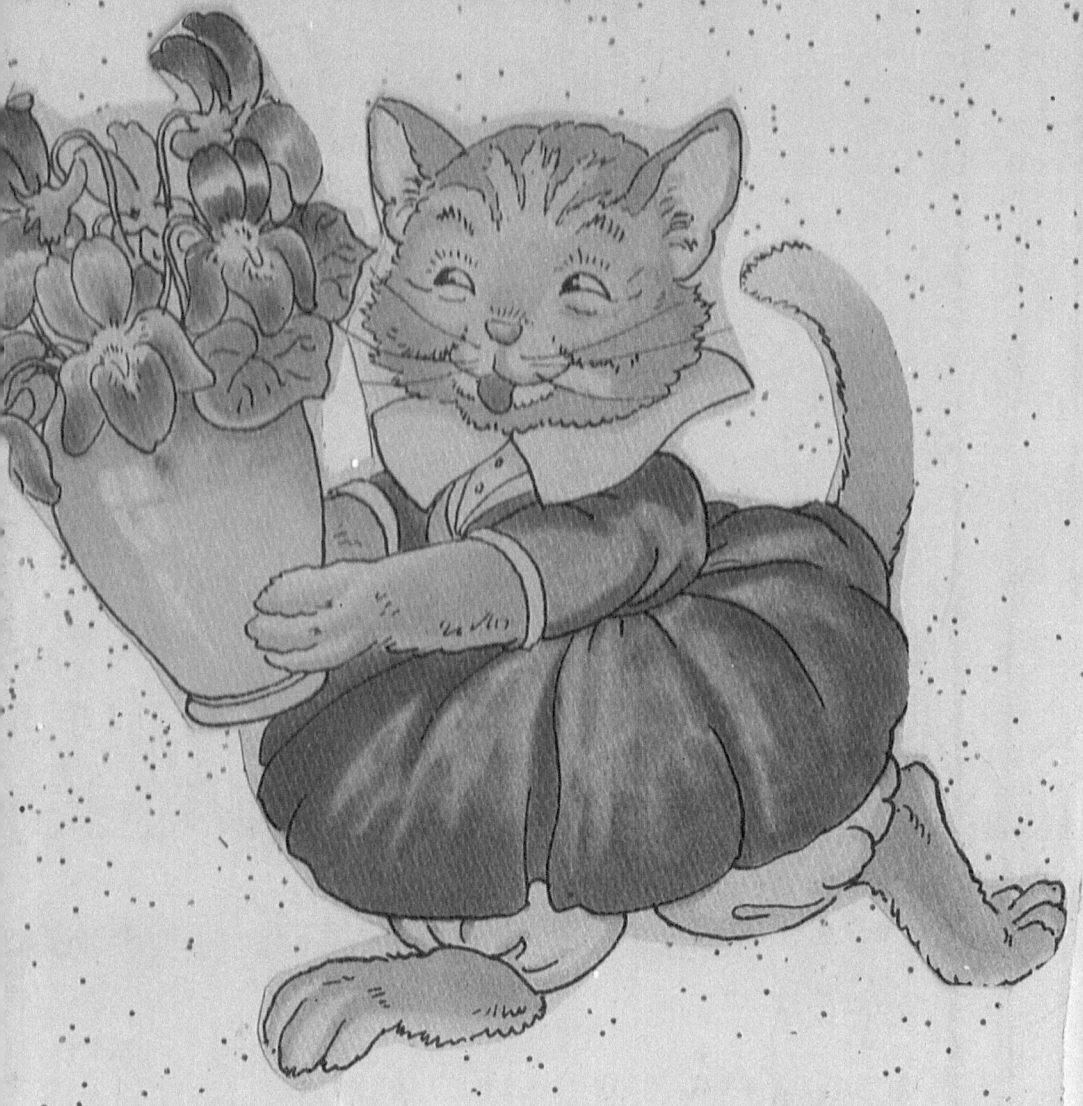

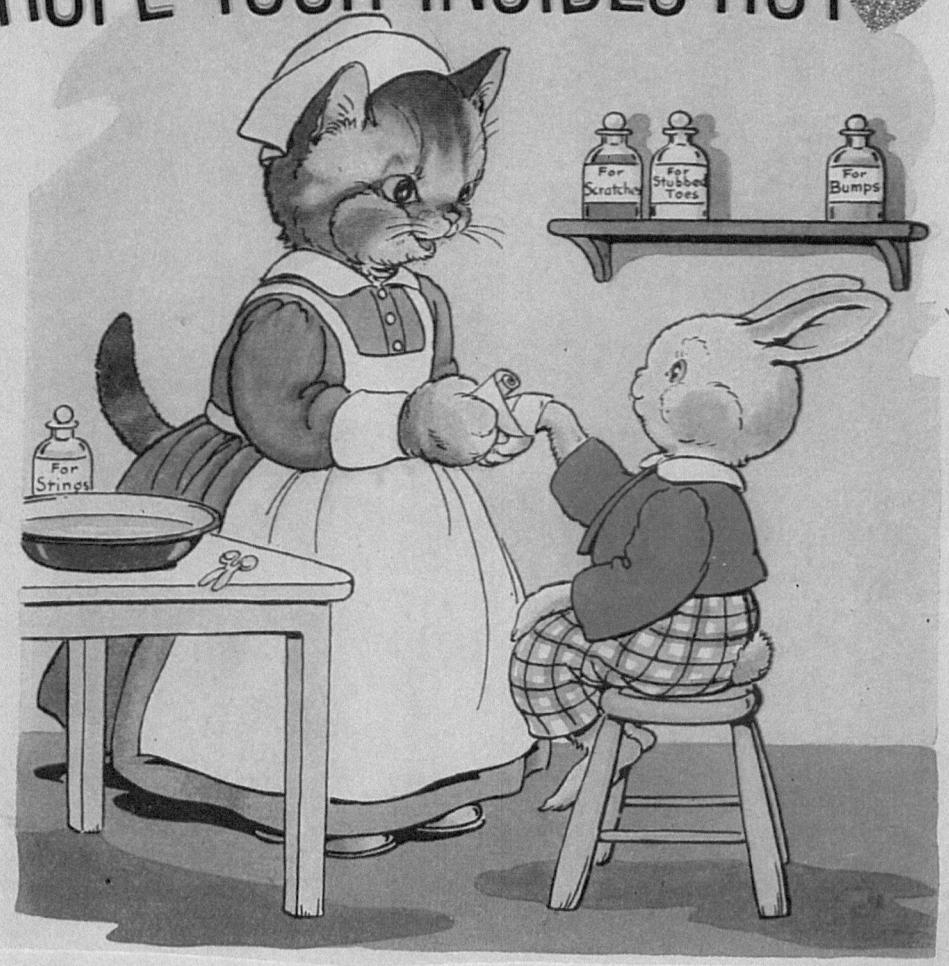

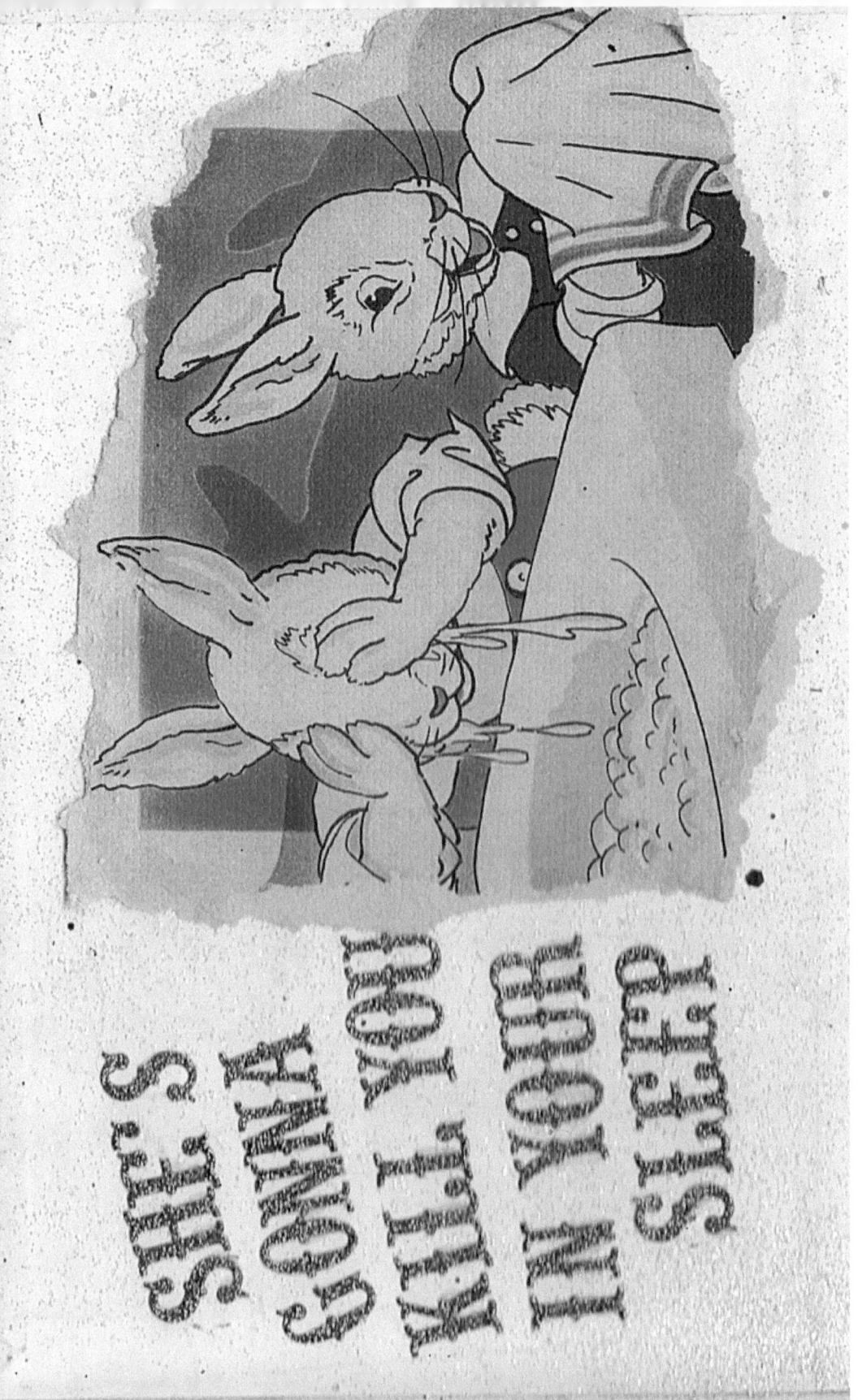

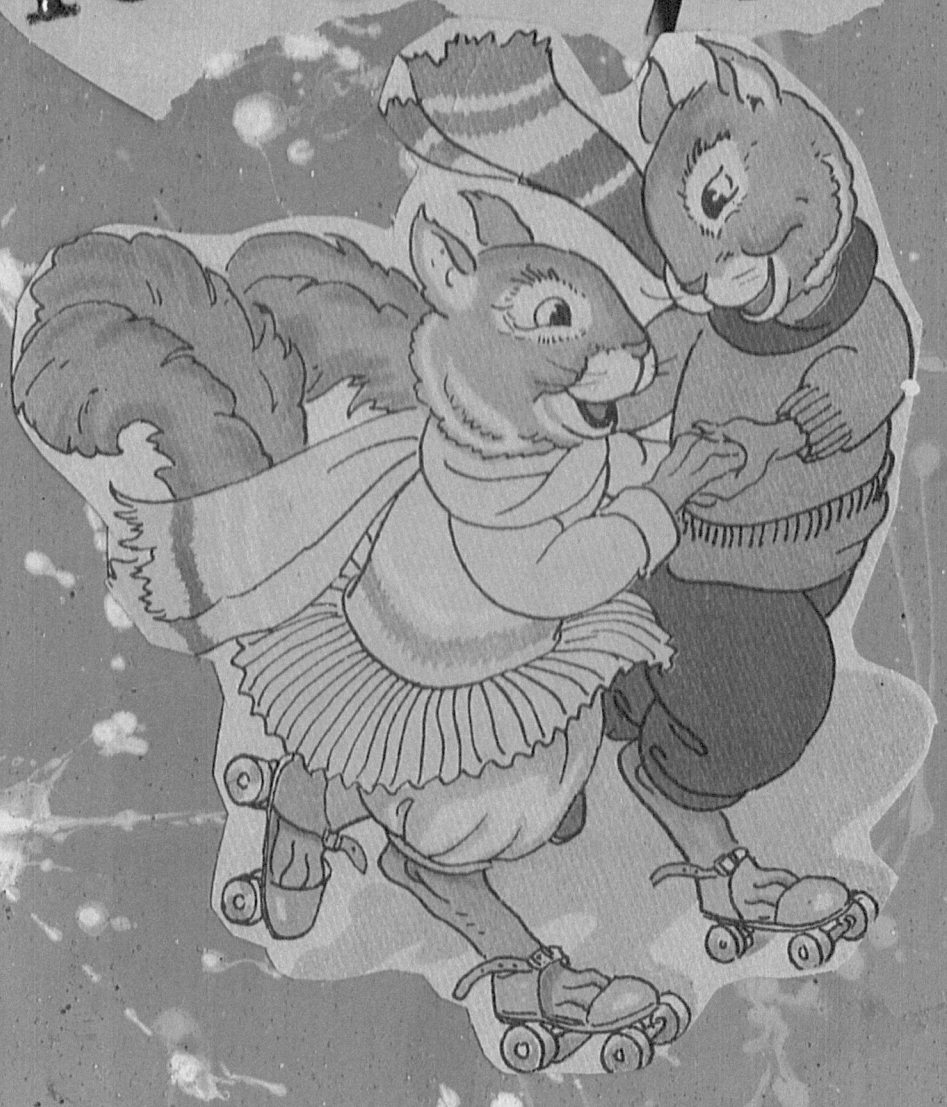

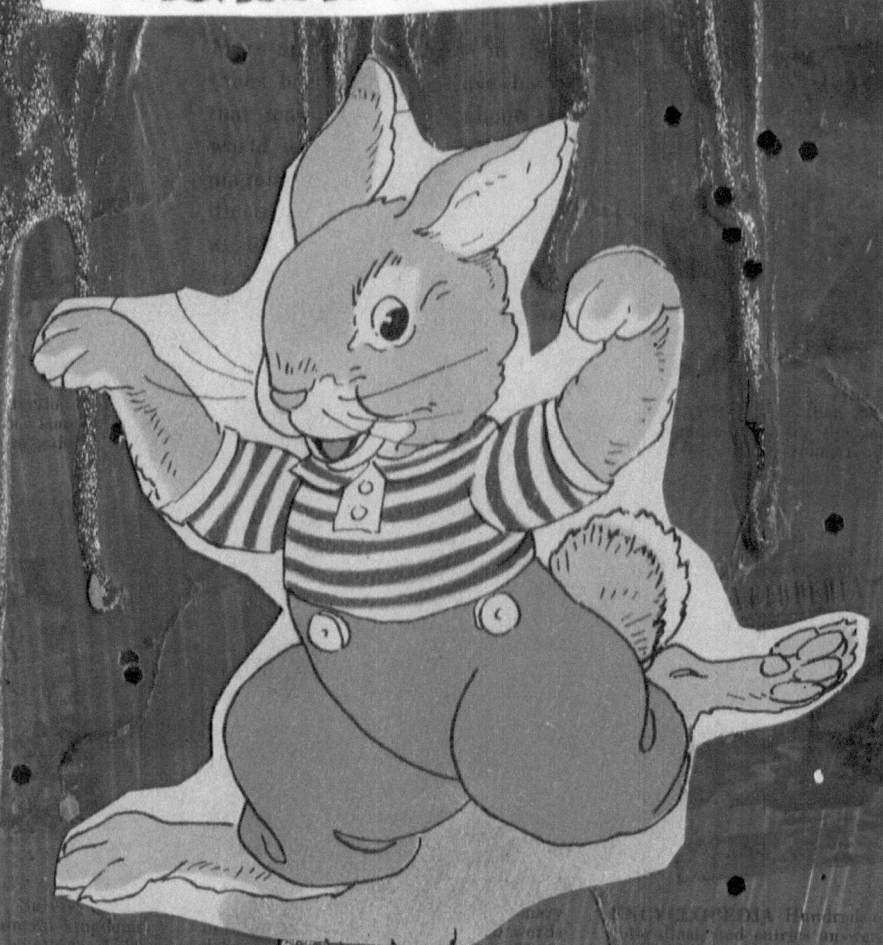

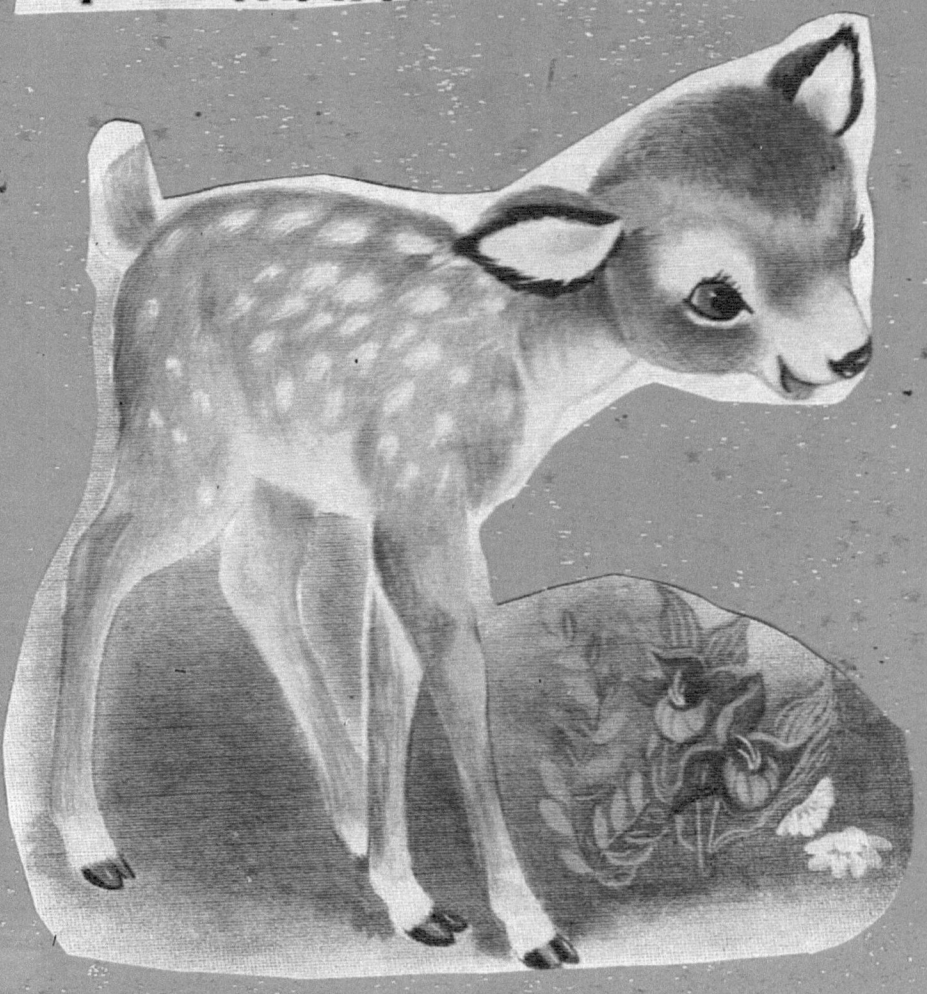

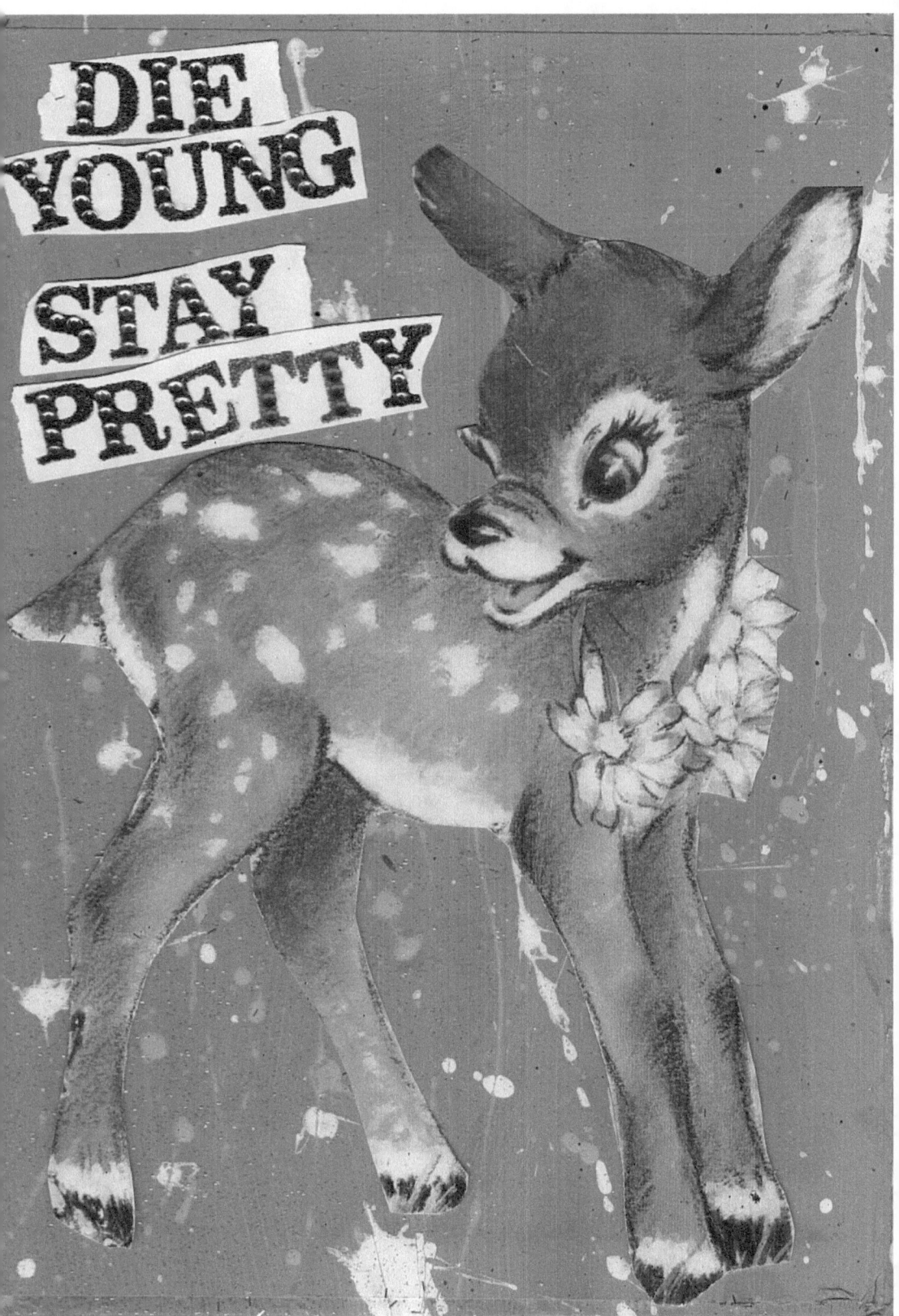

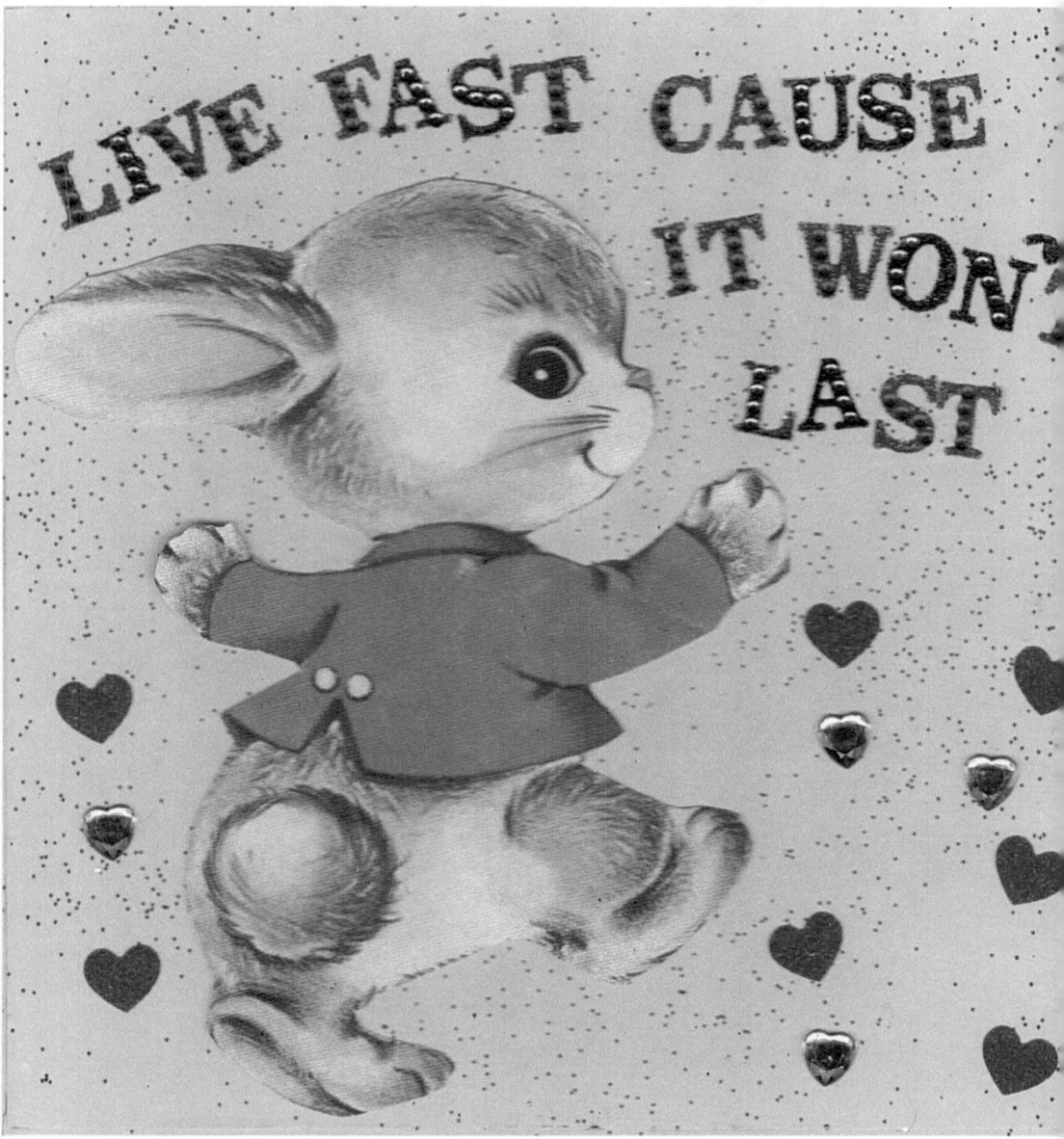

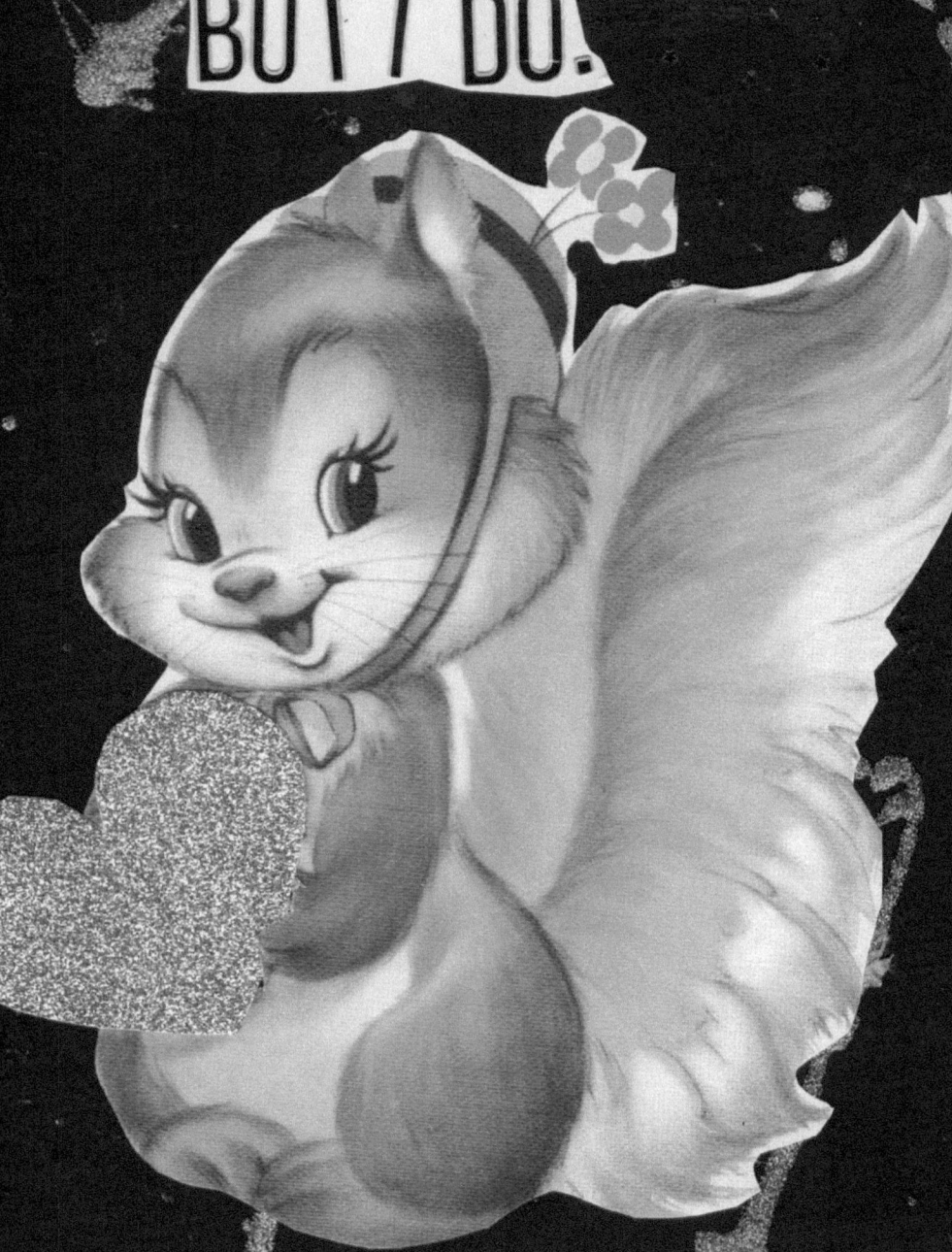

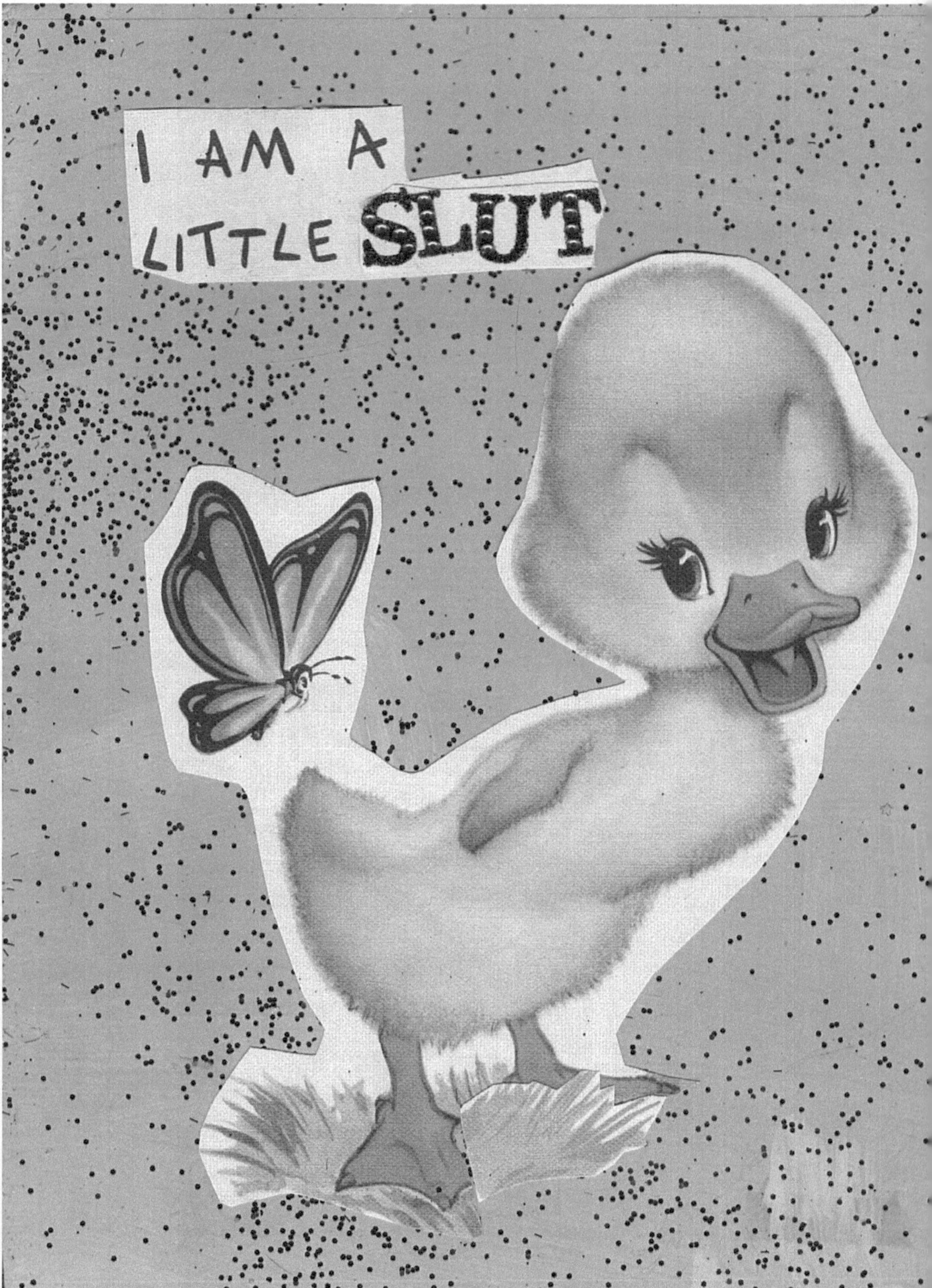
I AM A
LITTLE SLUT

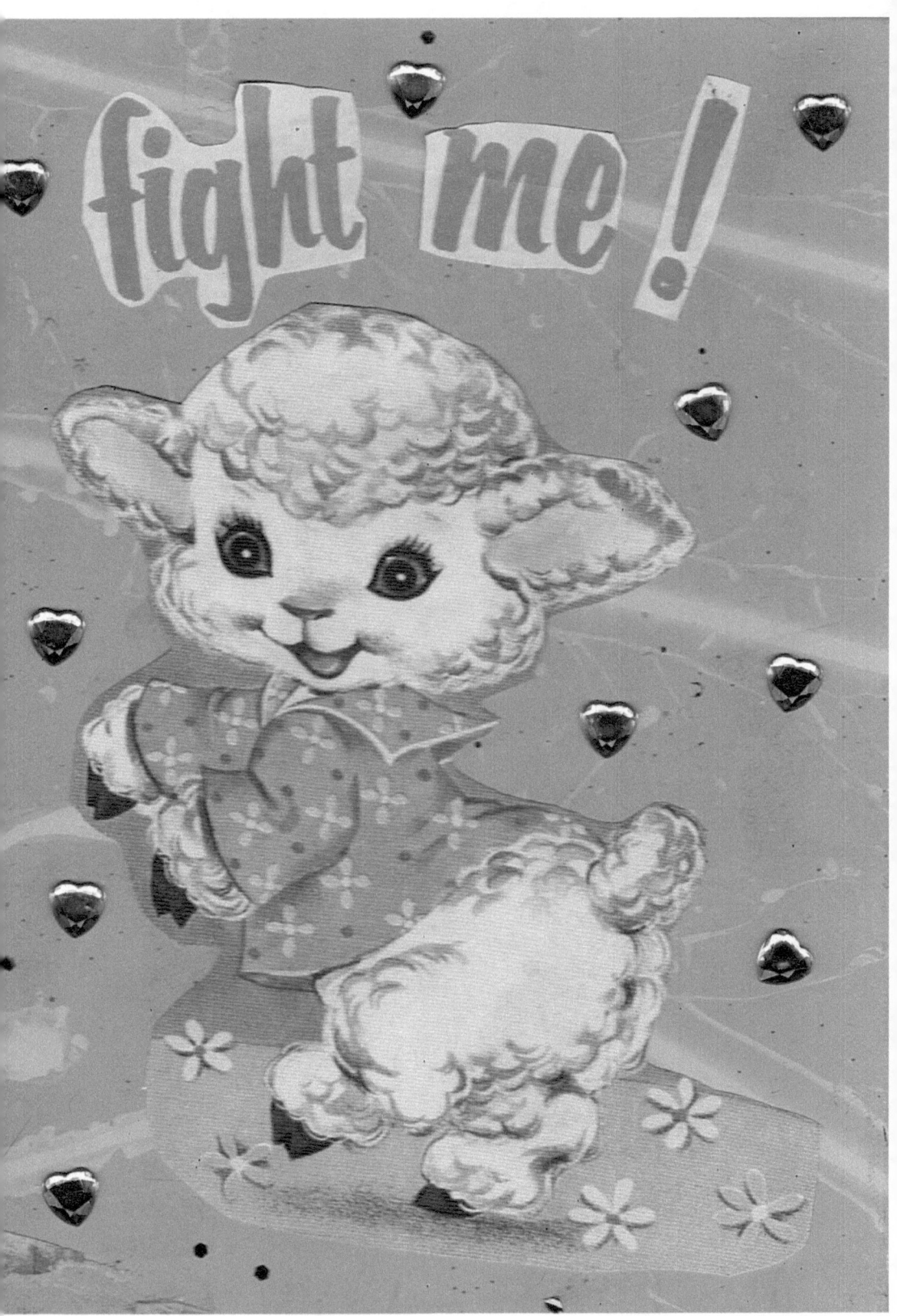

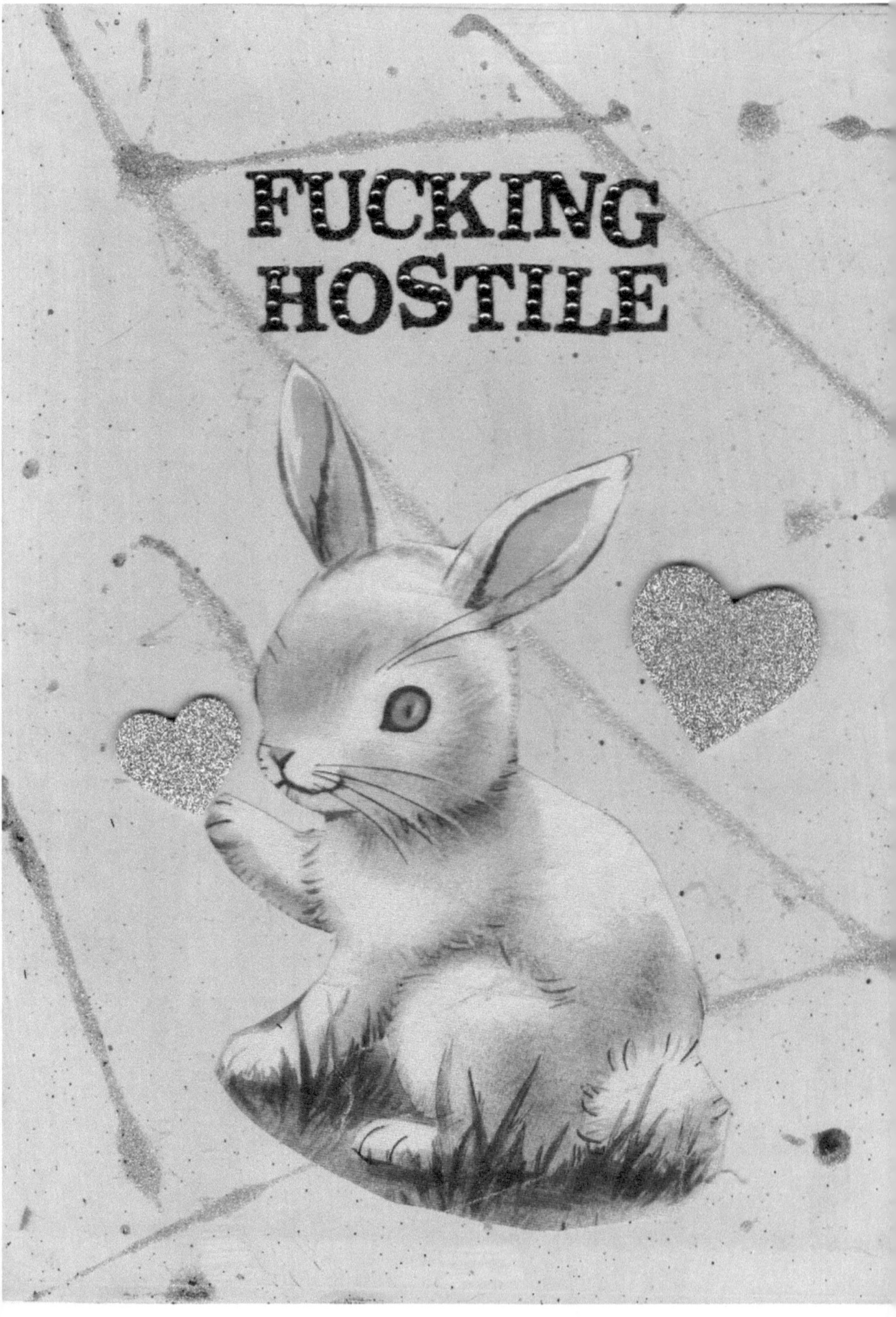

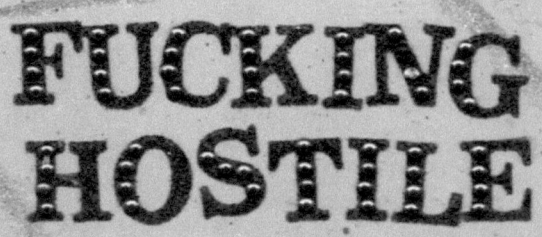

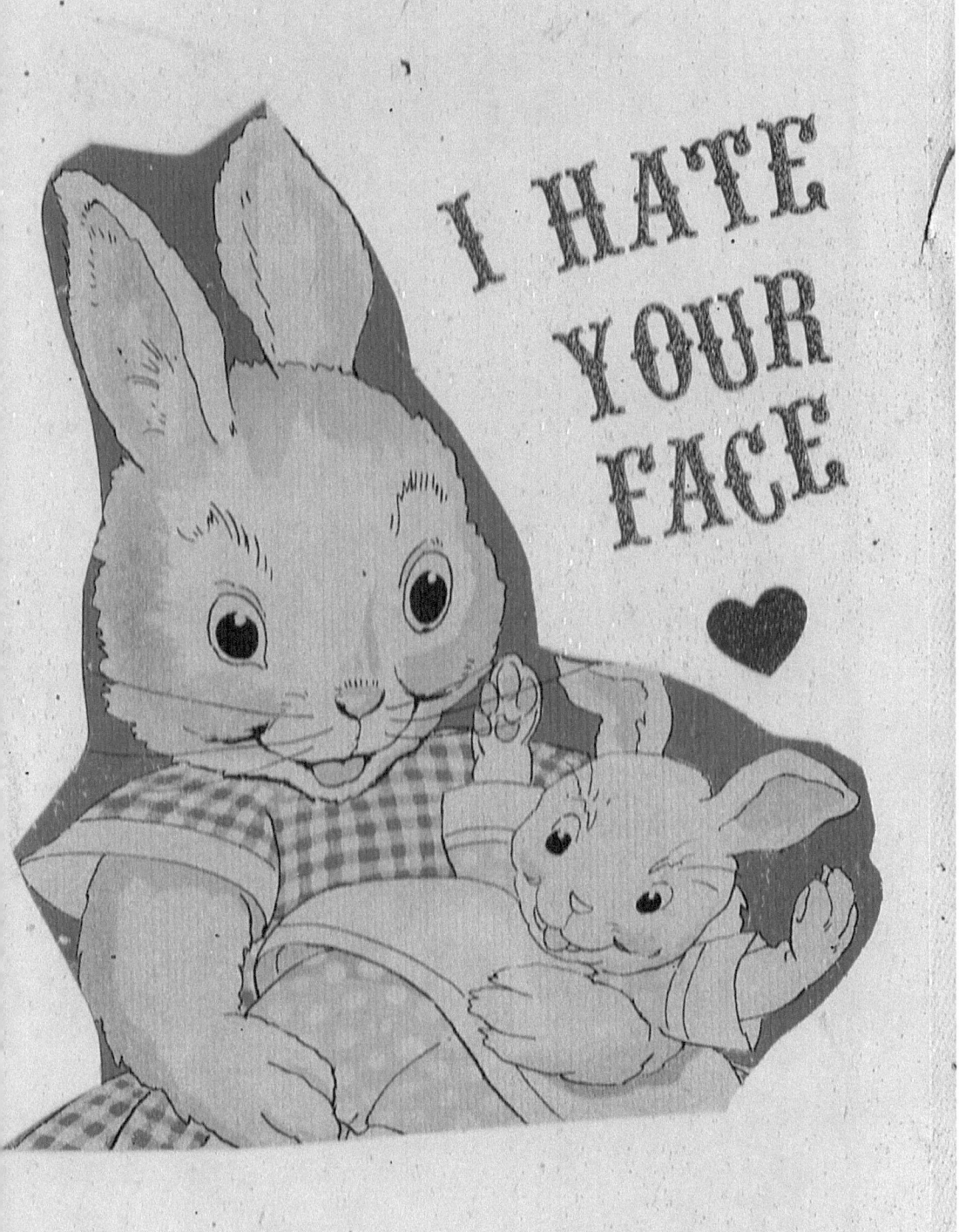

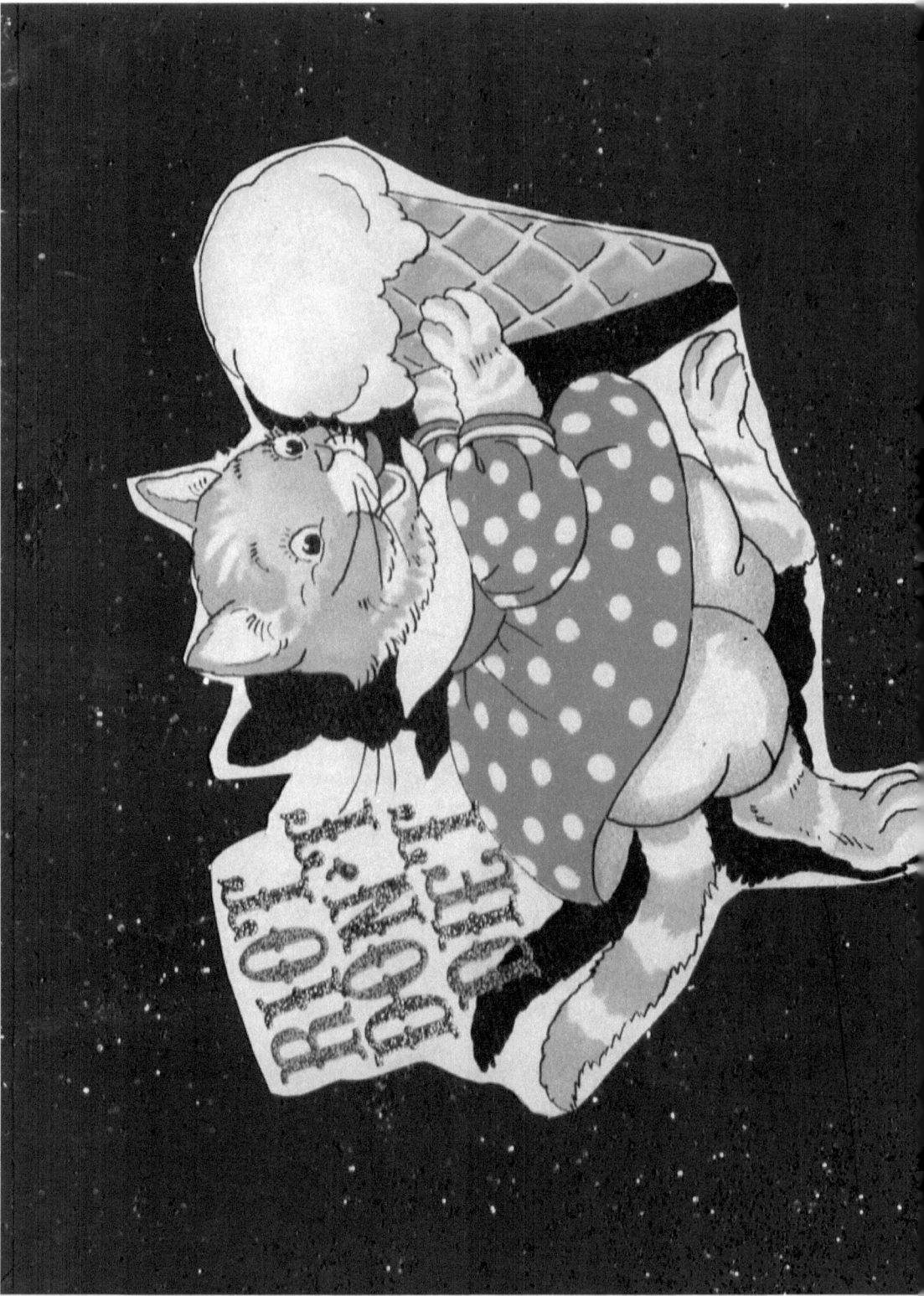

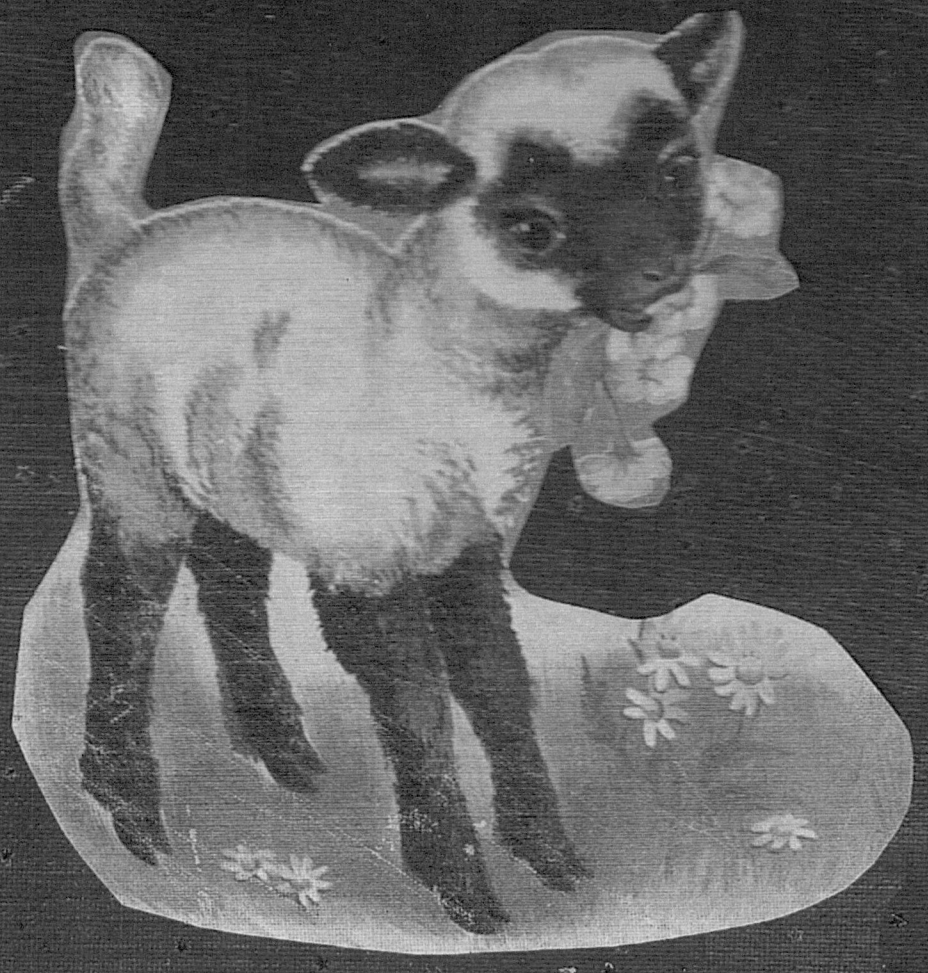

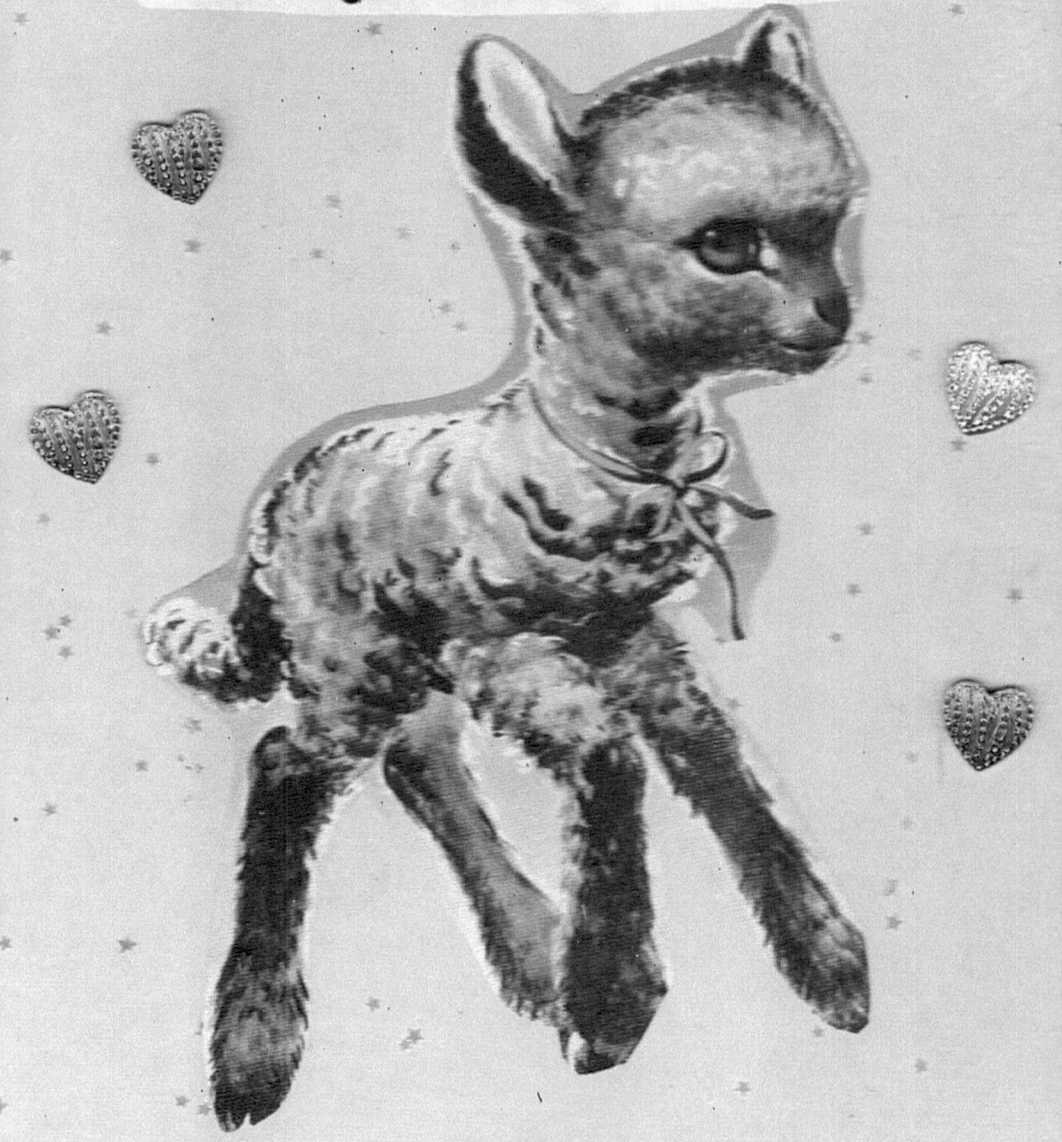

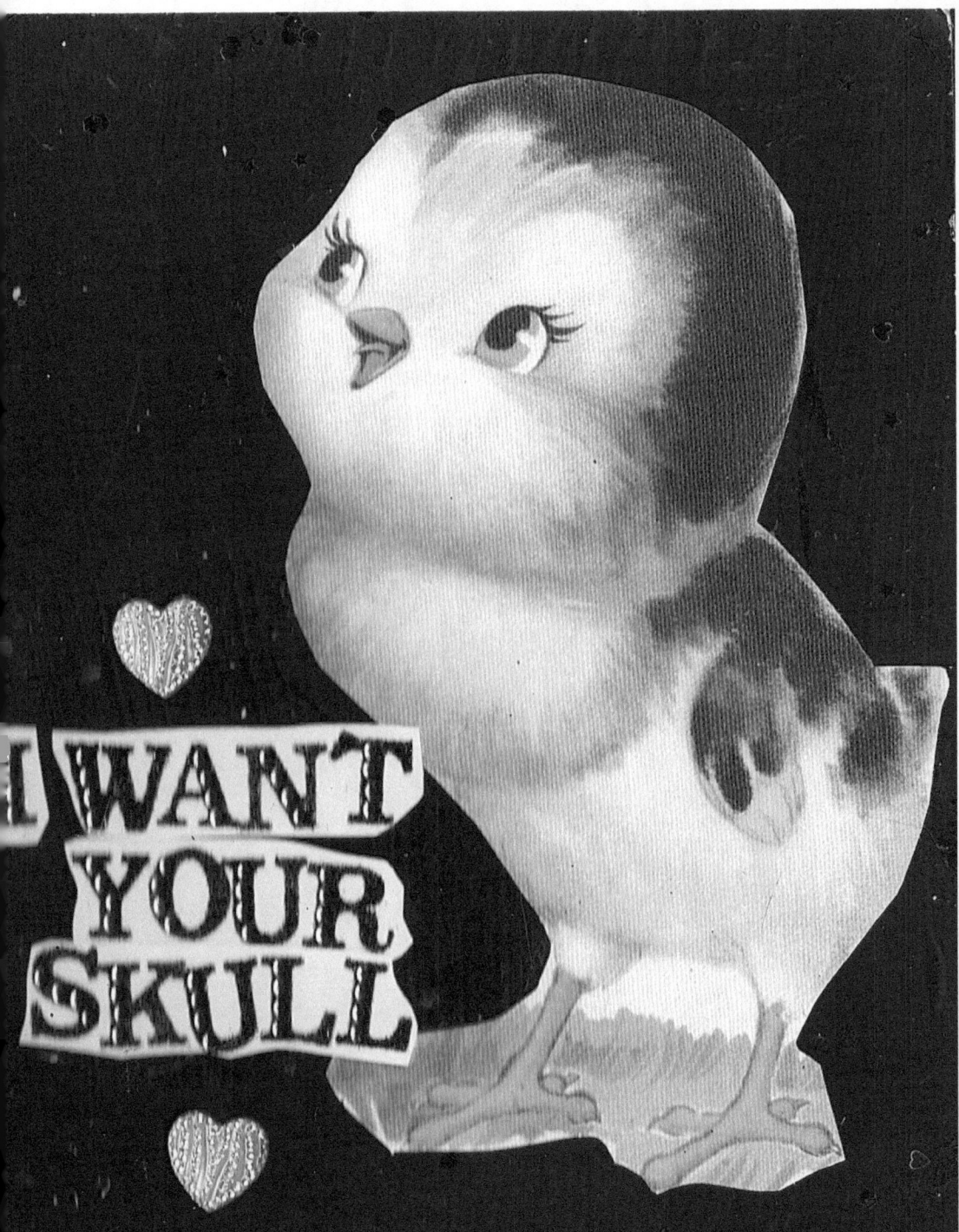

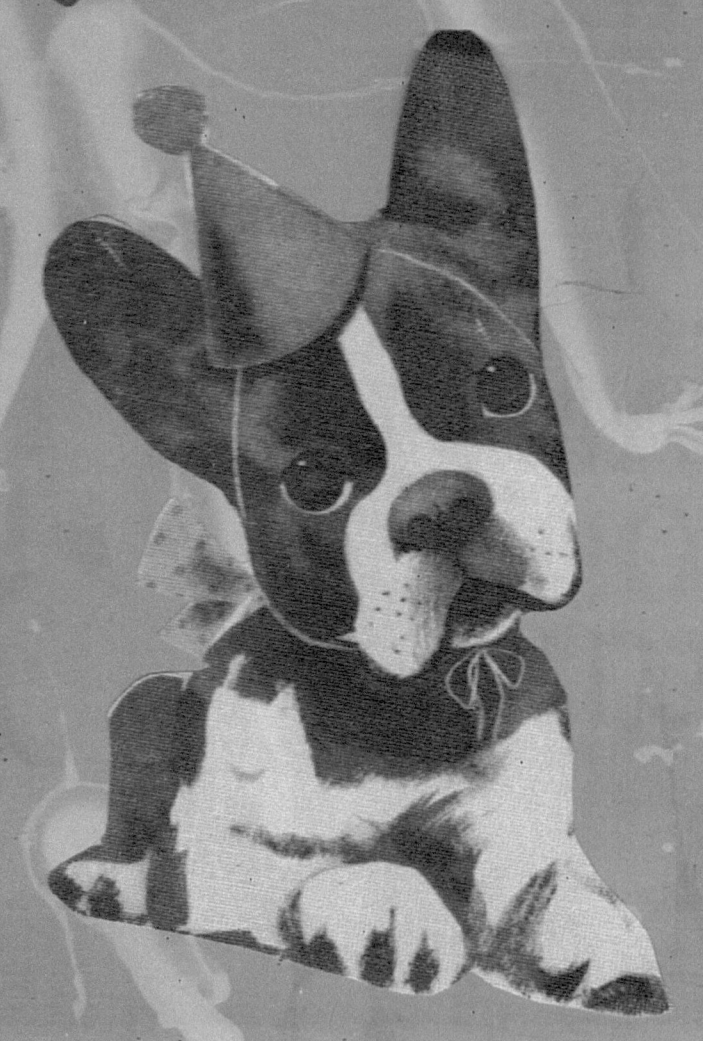

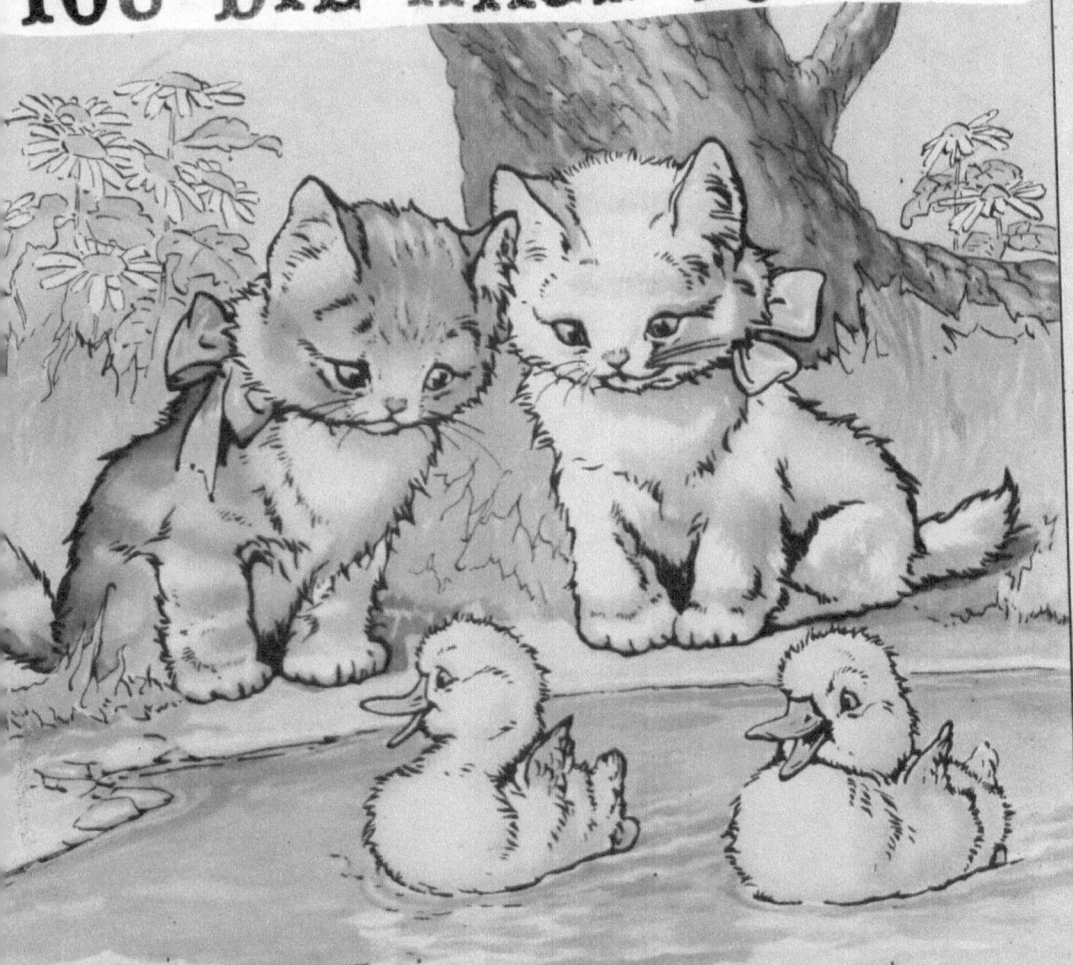

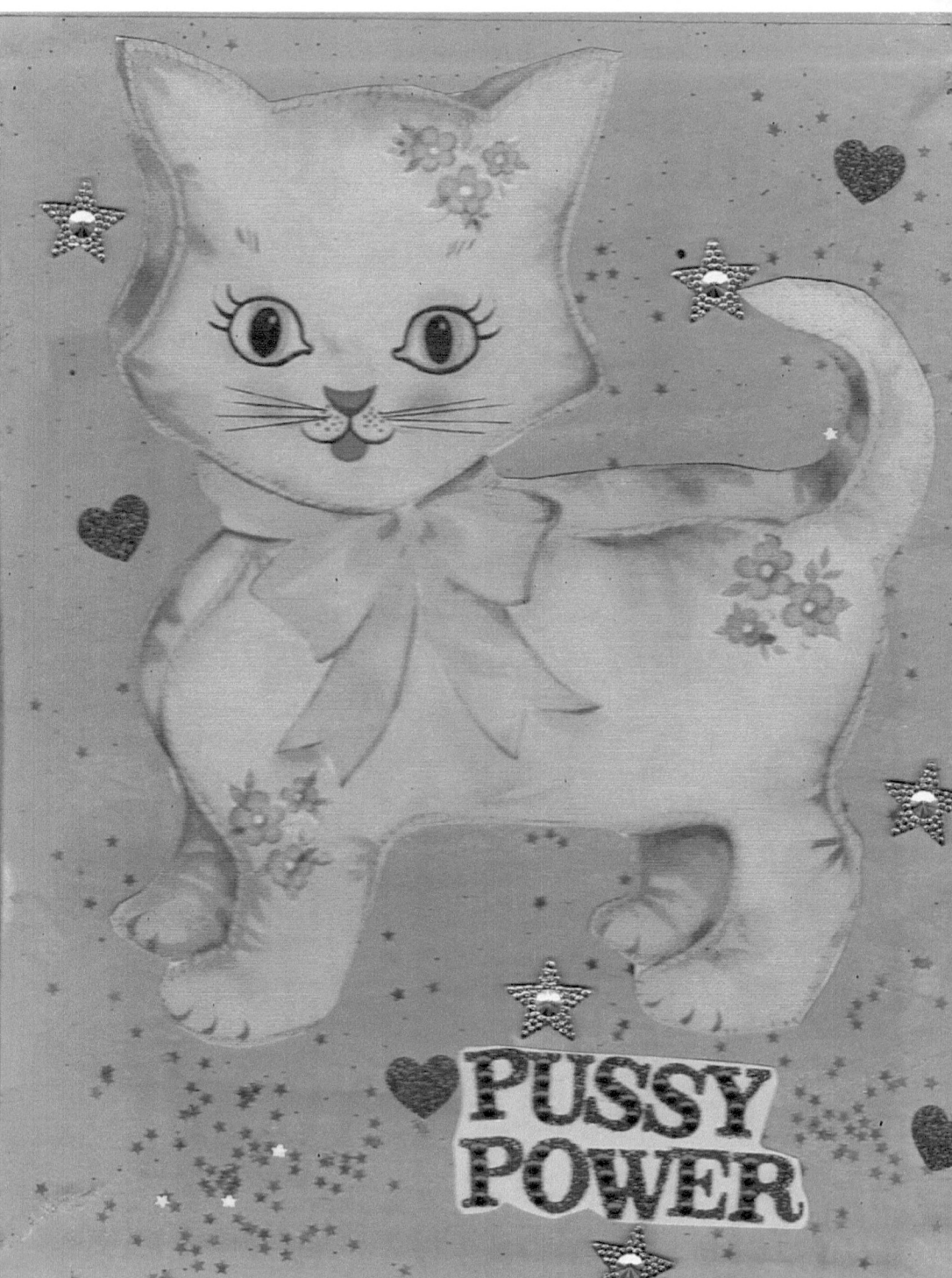

LIFE
SUCKS
EAT
DRUGS

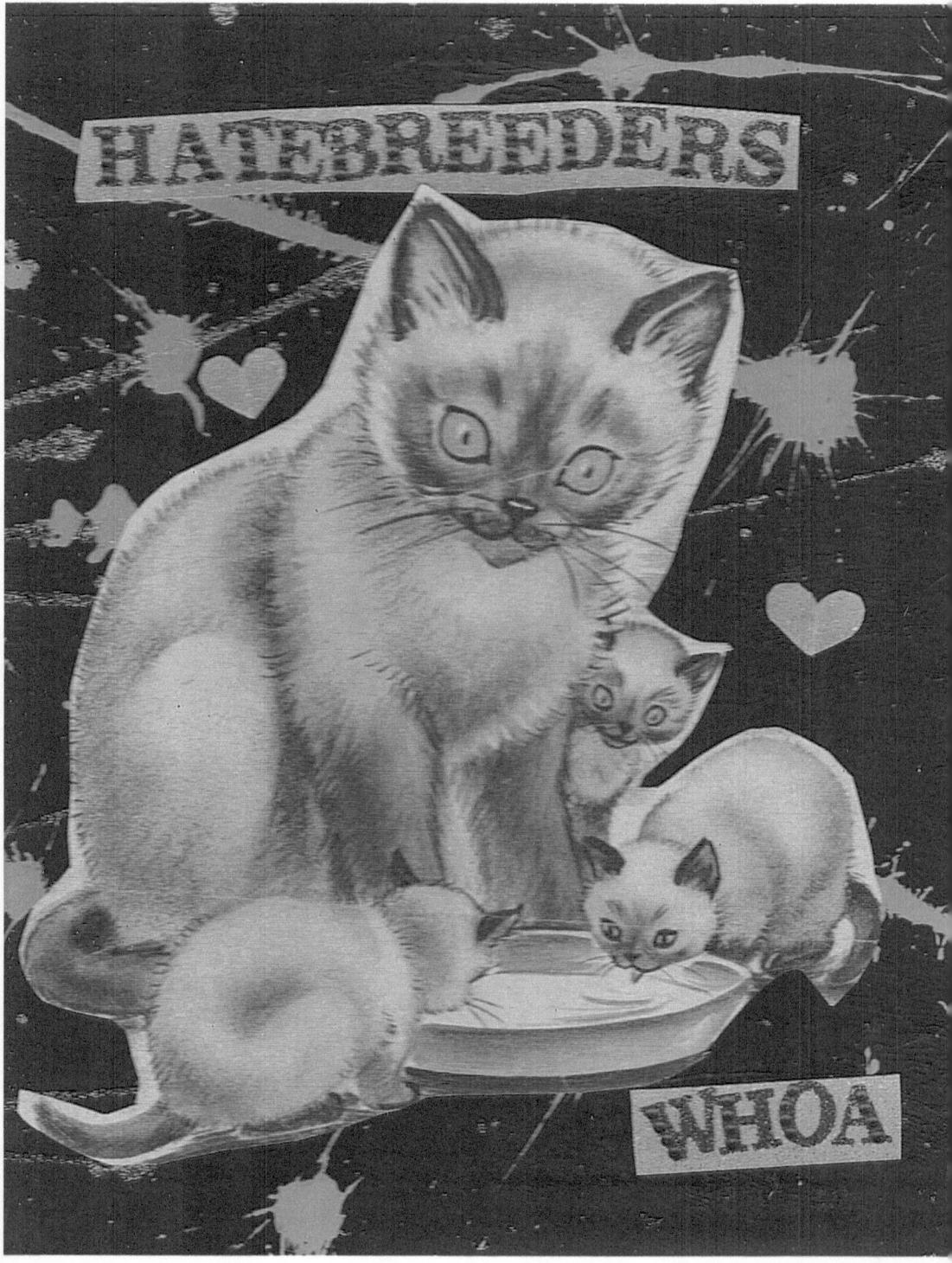

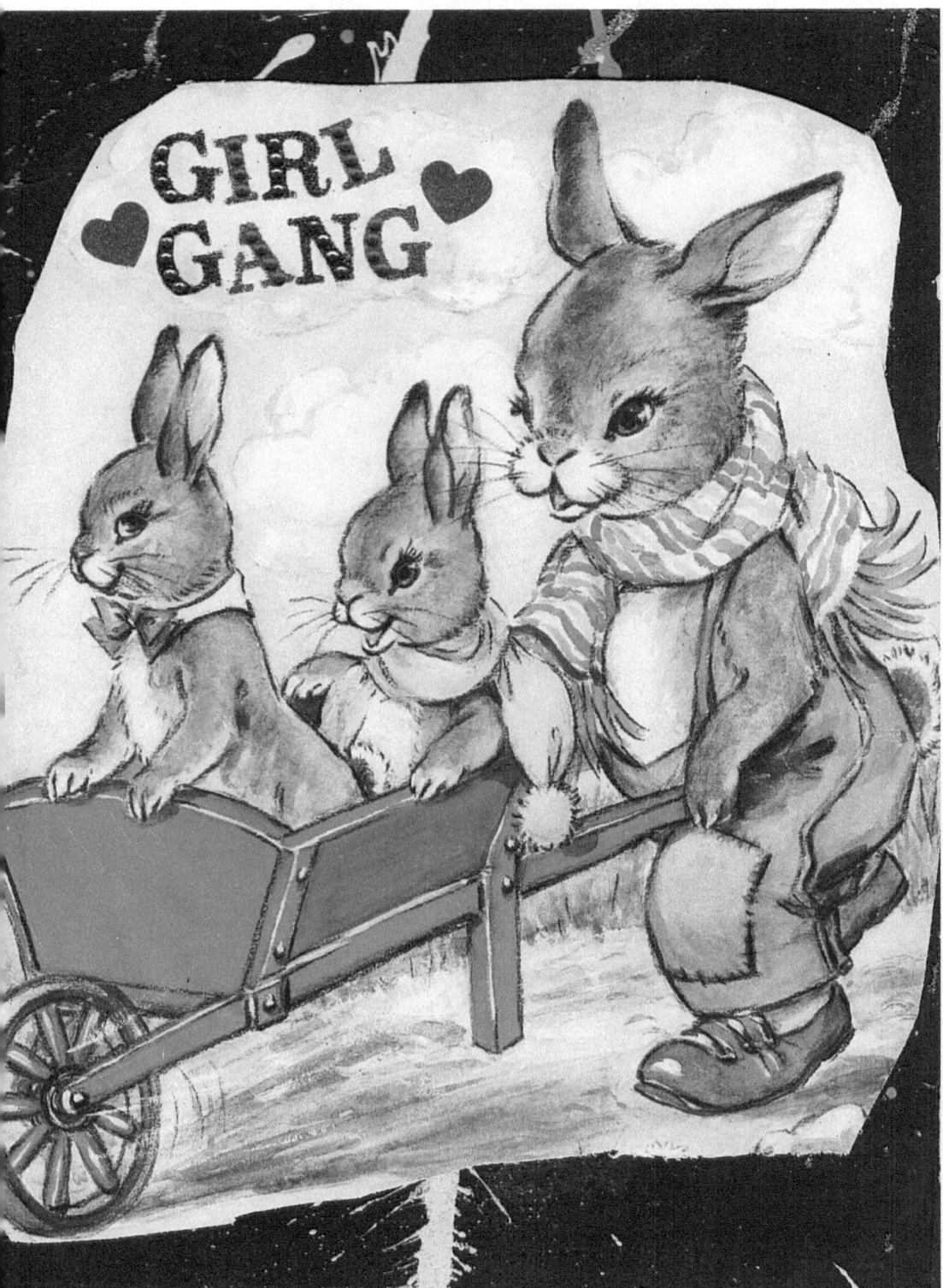

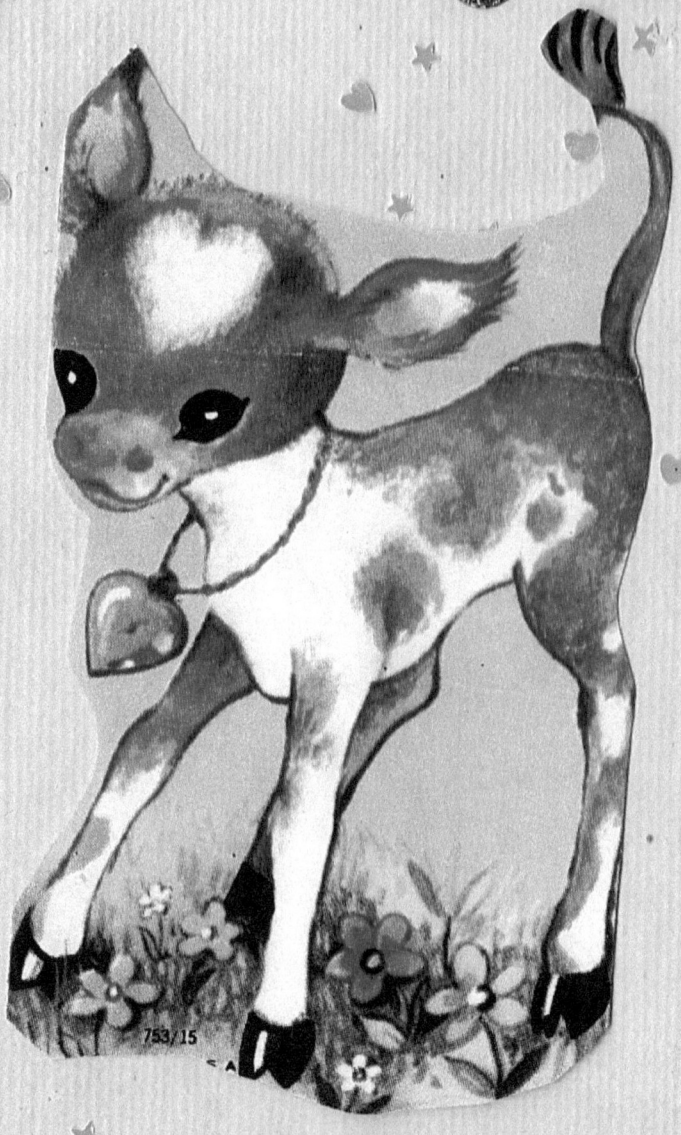

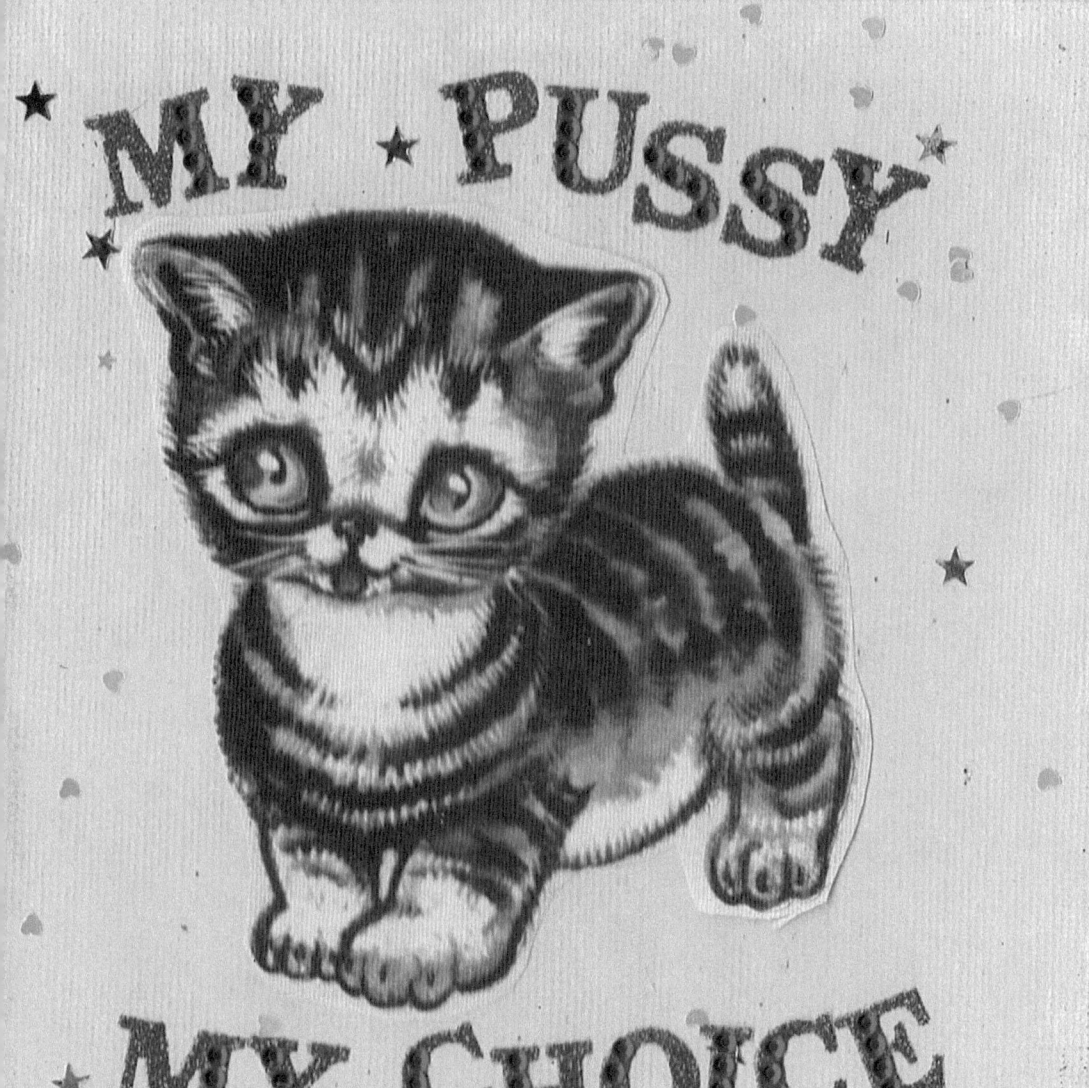

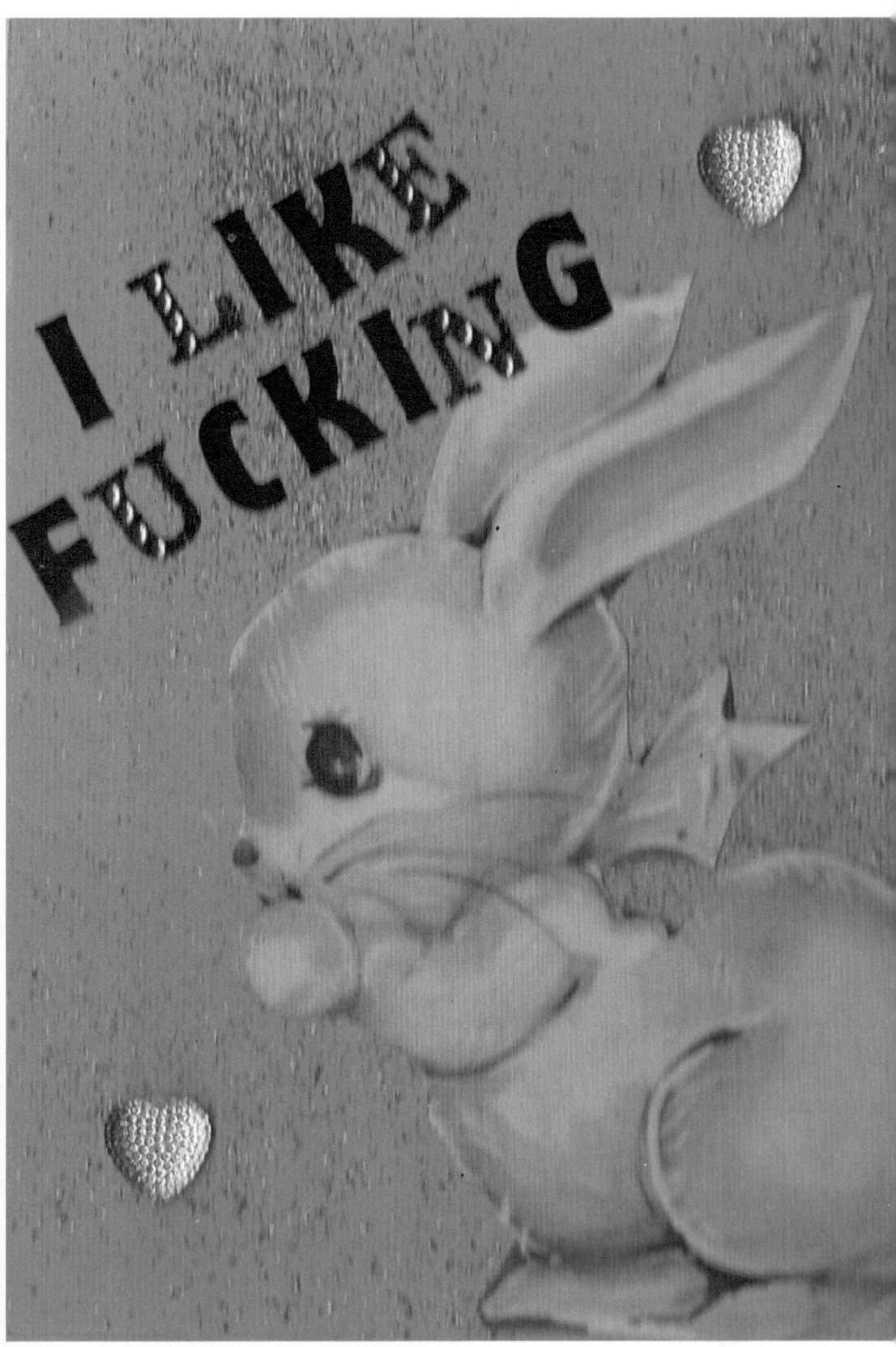

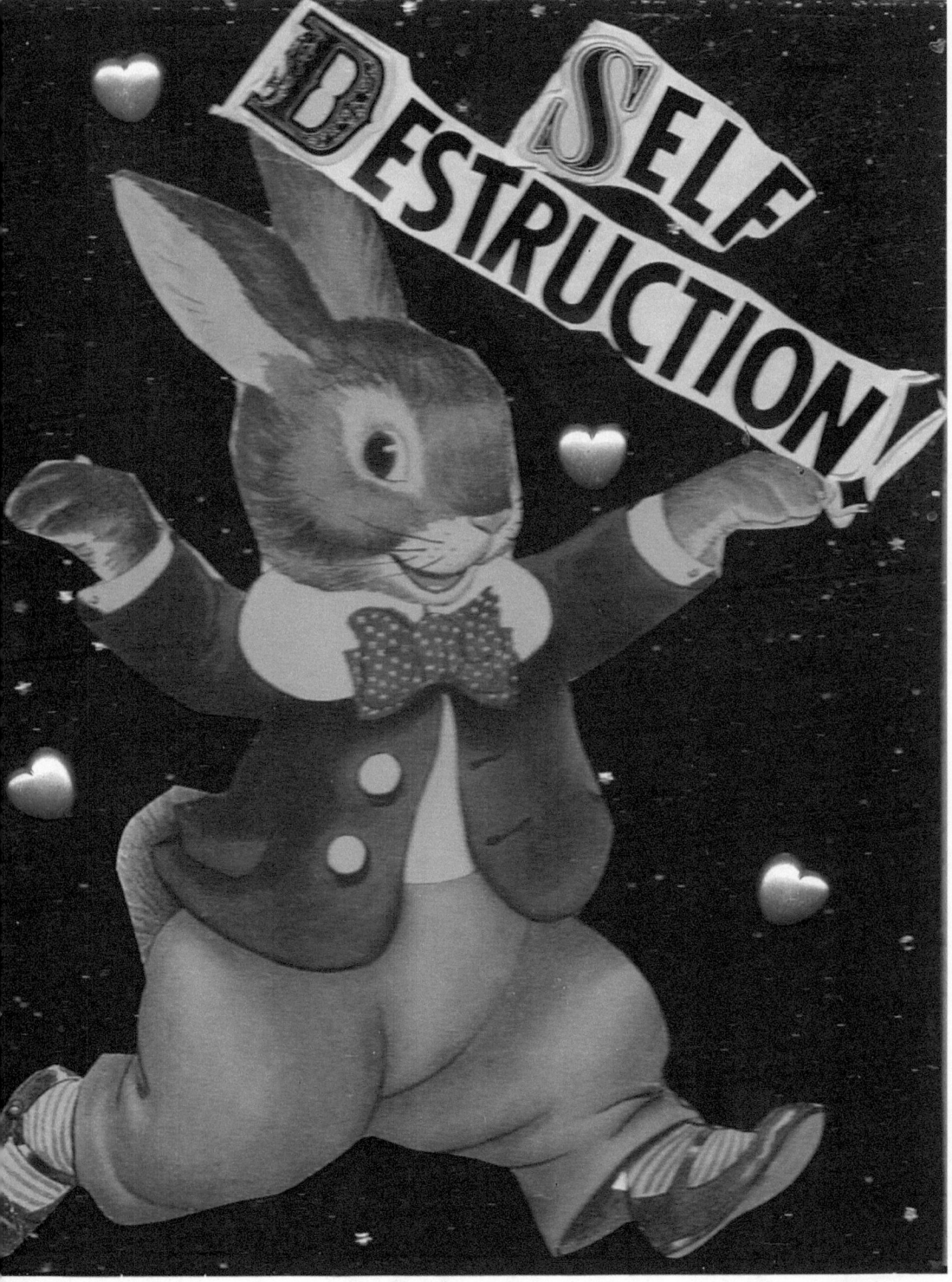

WE SAVAGES DON'T NEED A SAINT

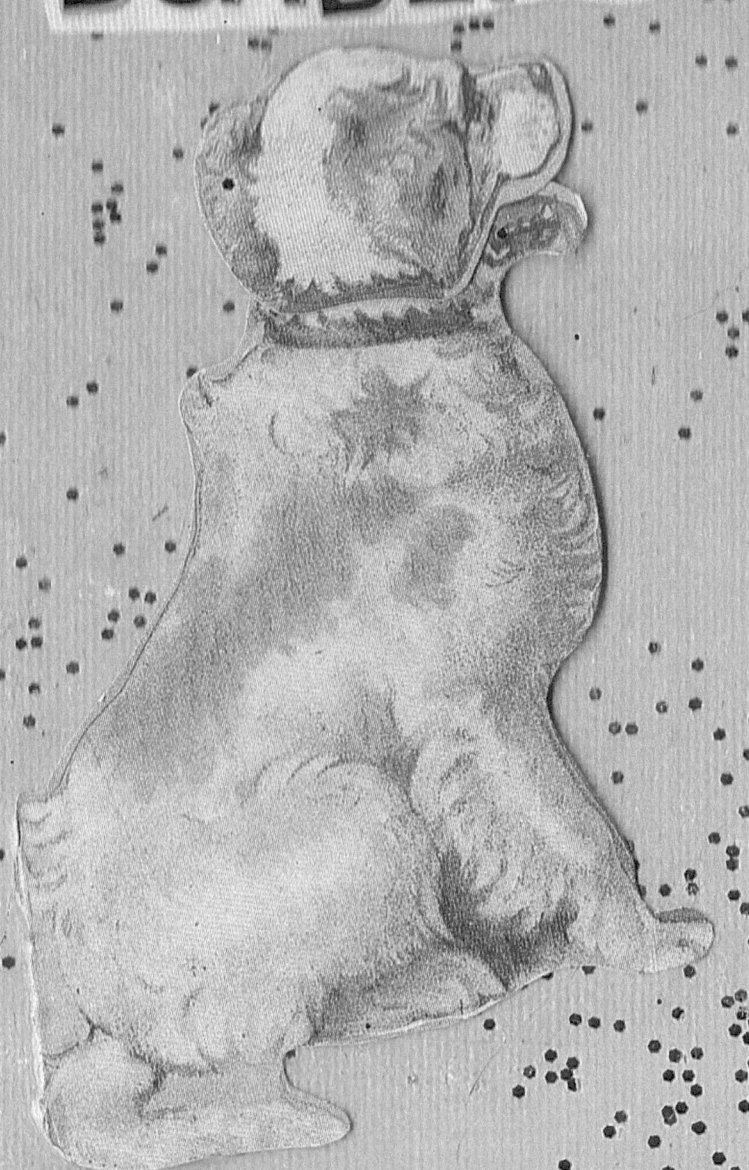

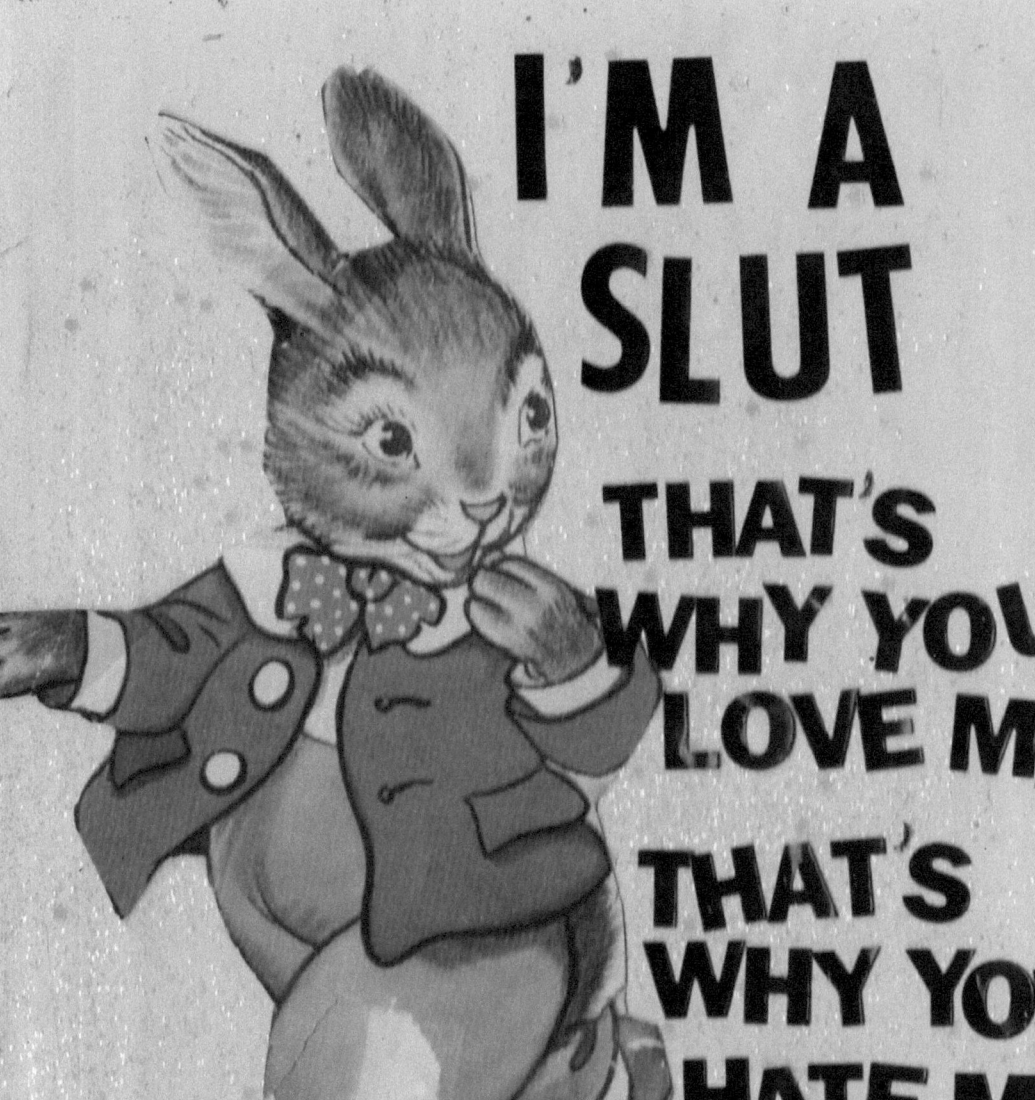

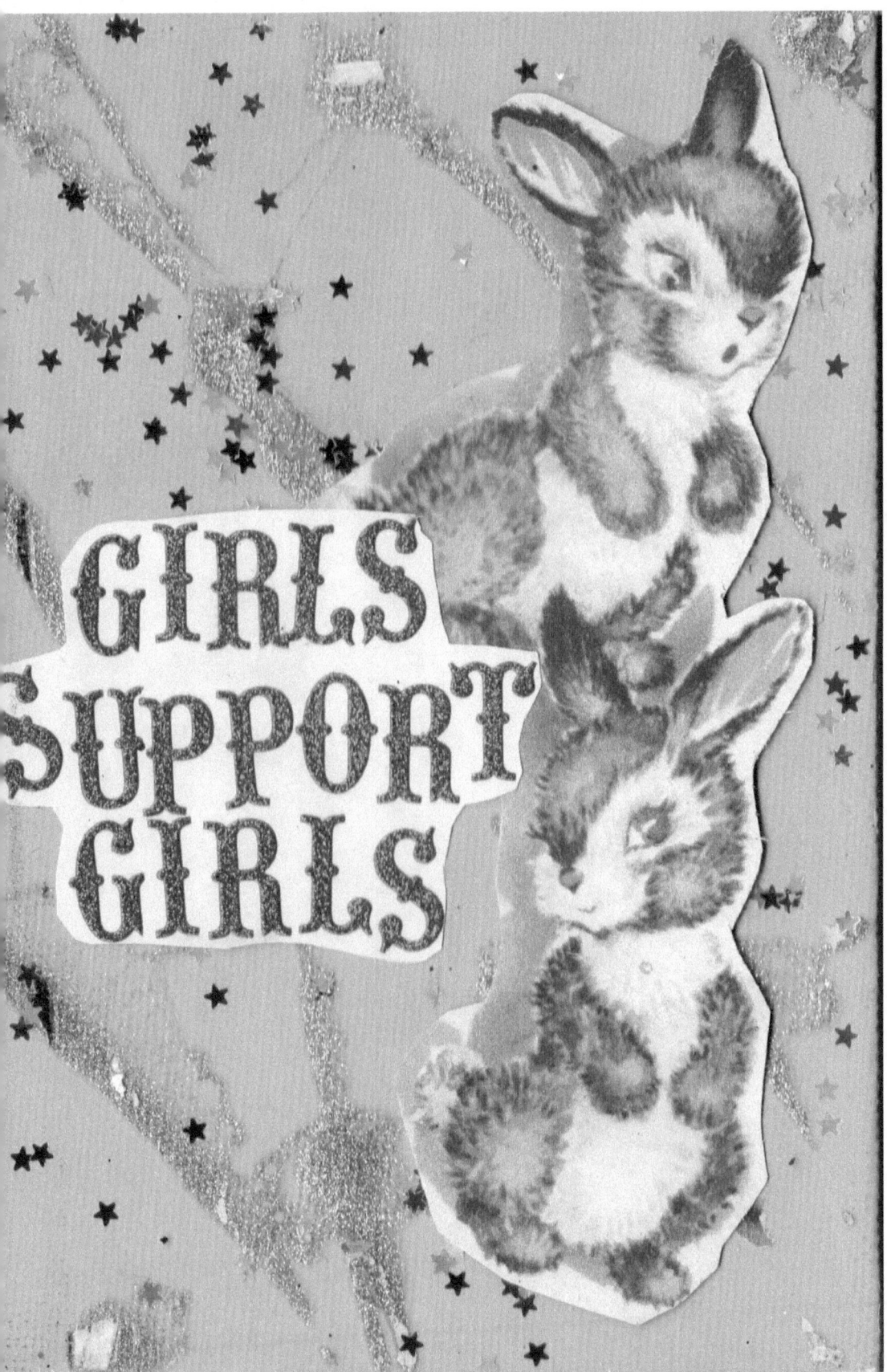

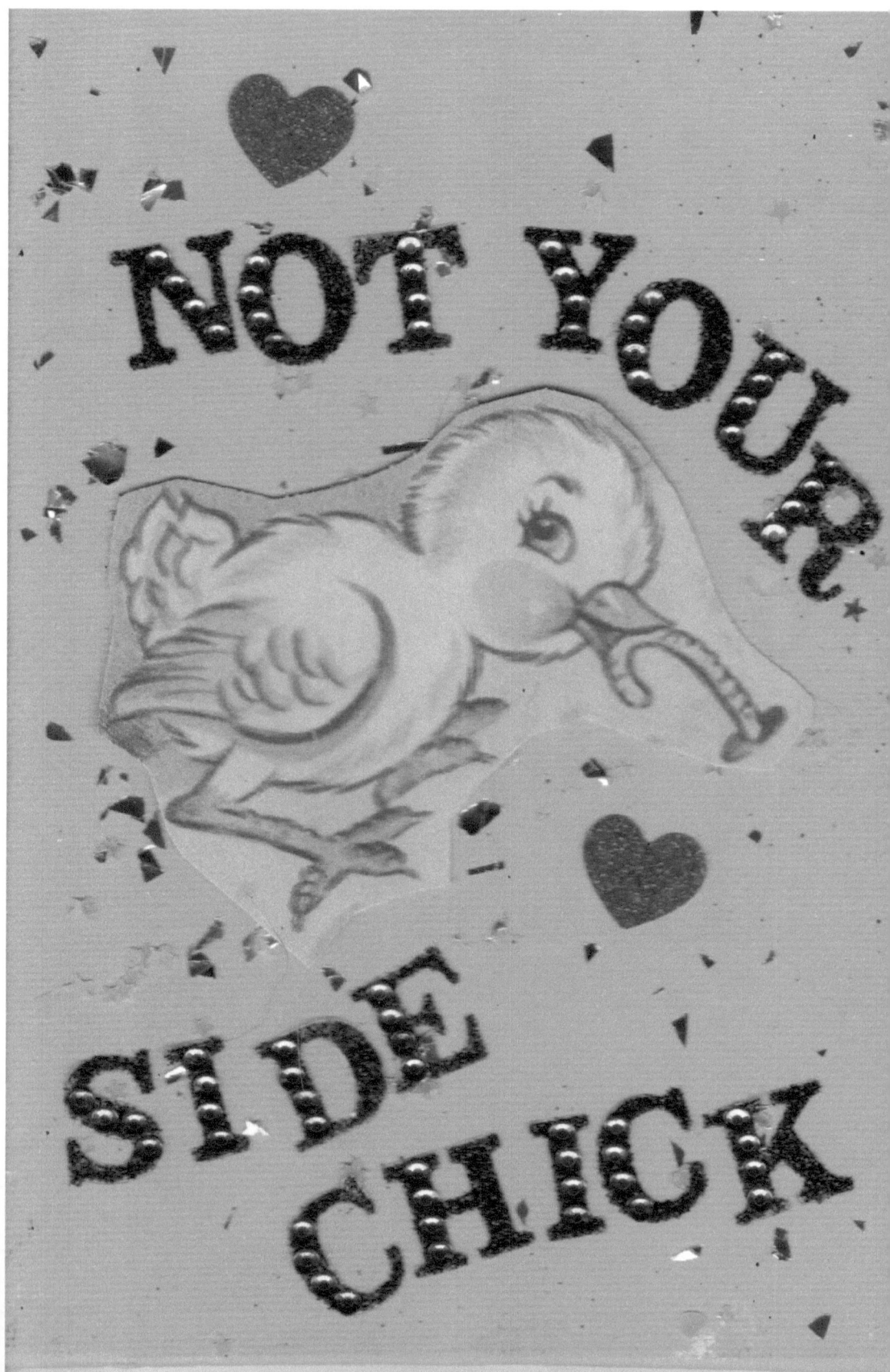

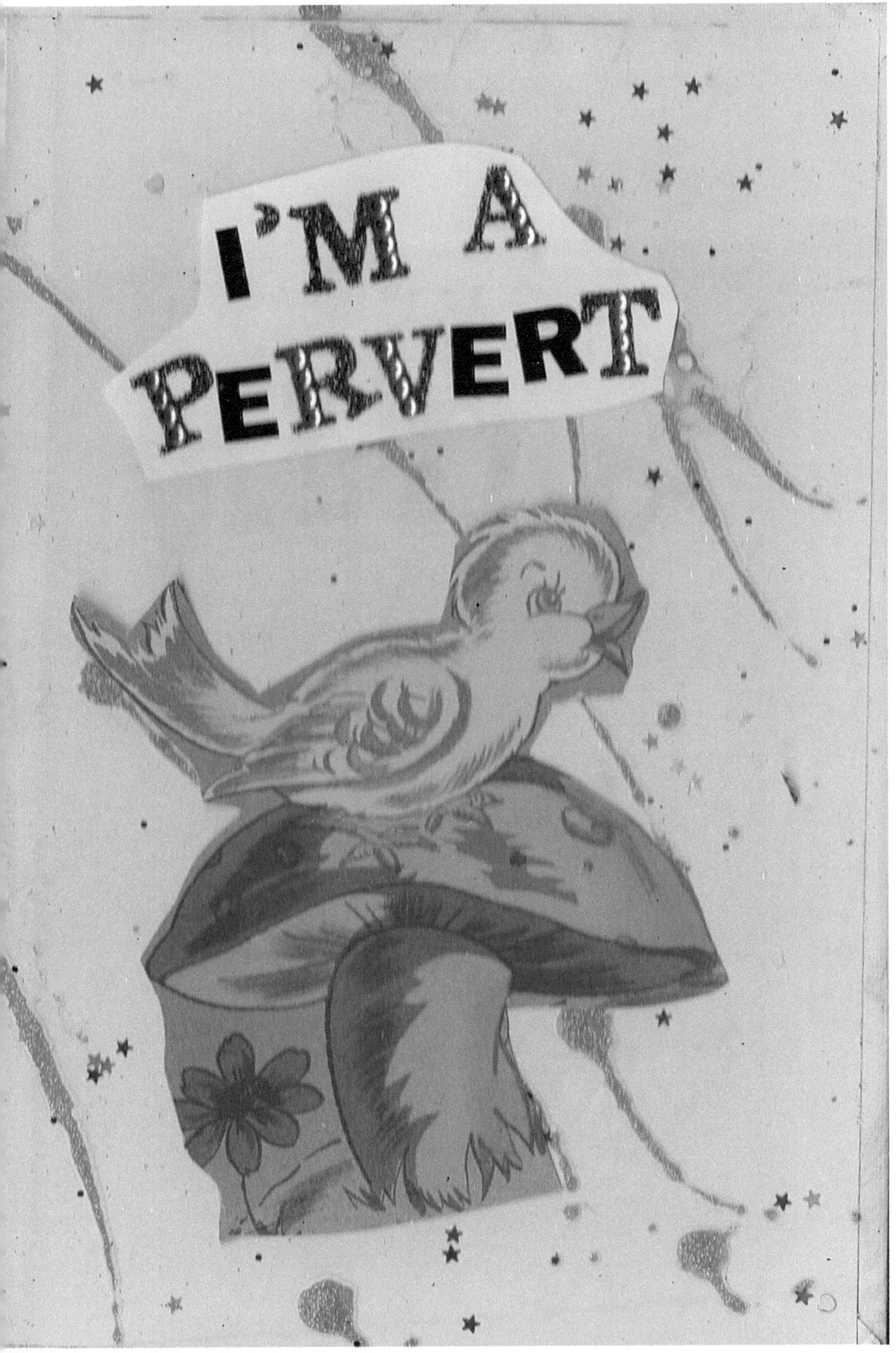
I'M A
PERVERT

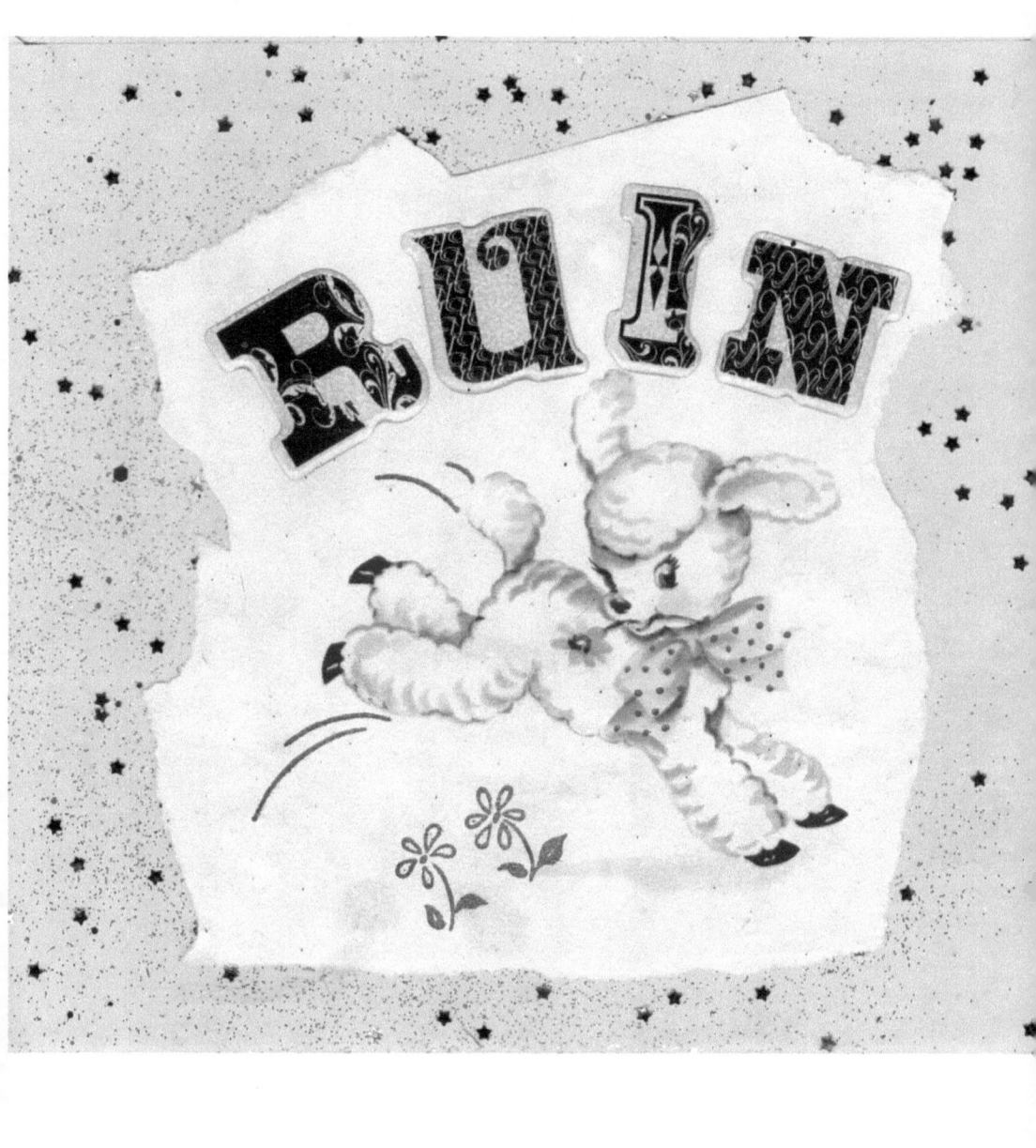

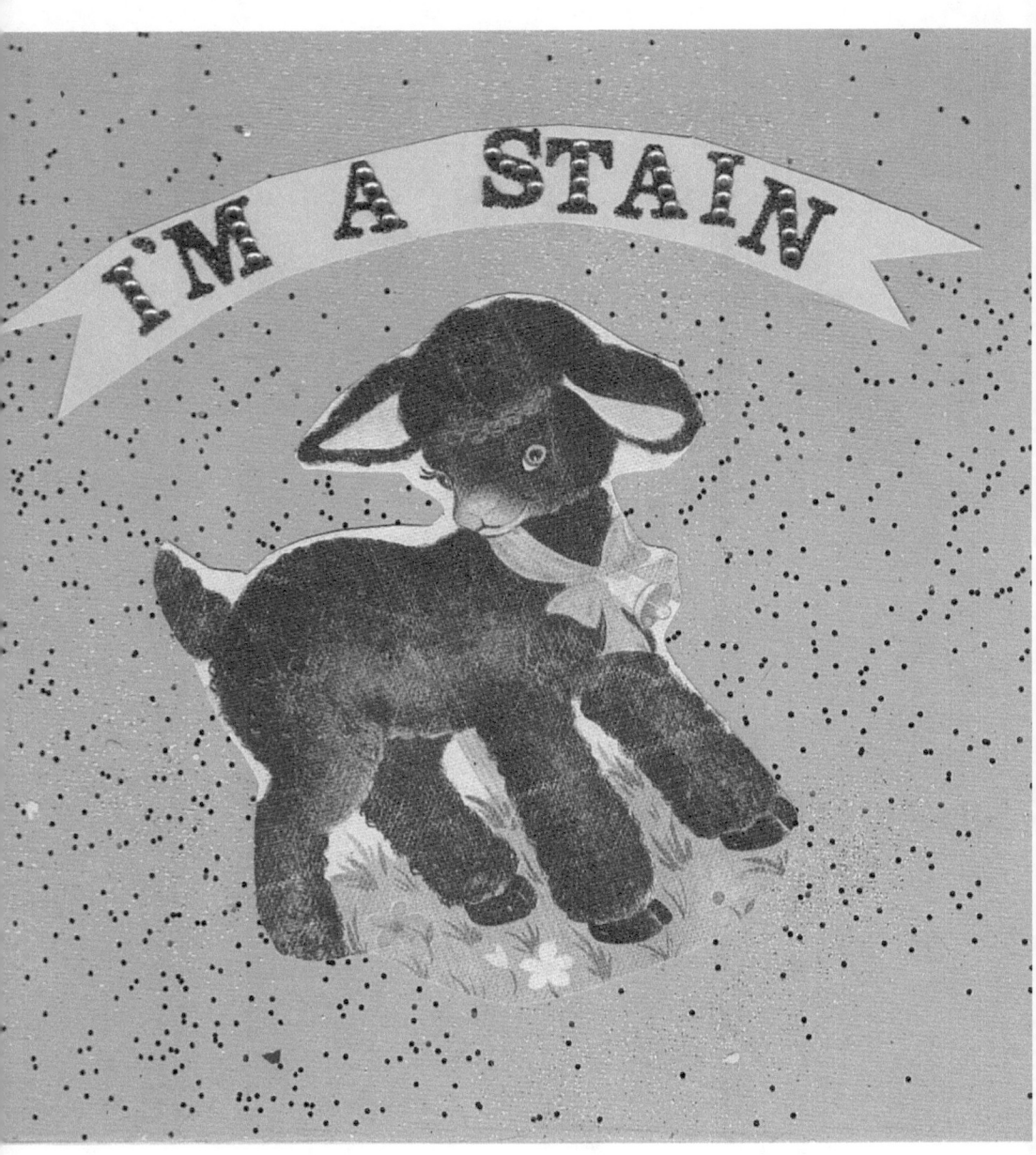

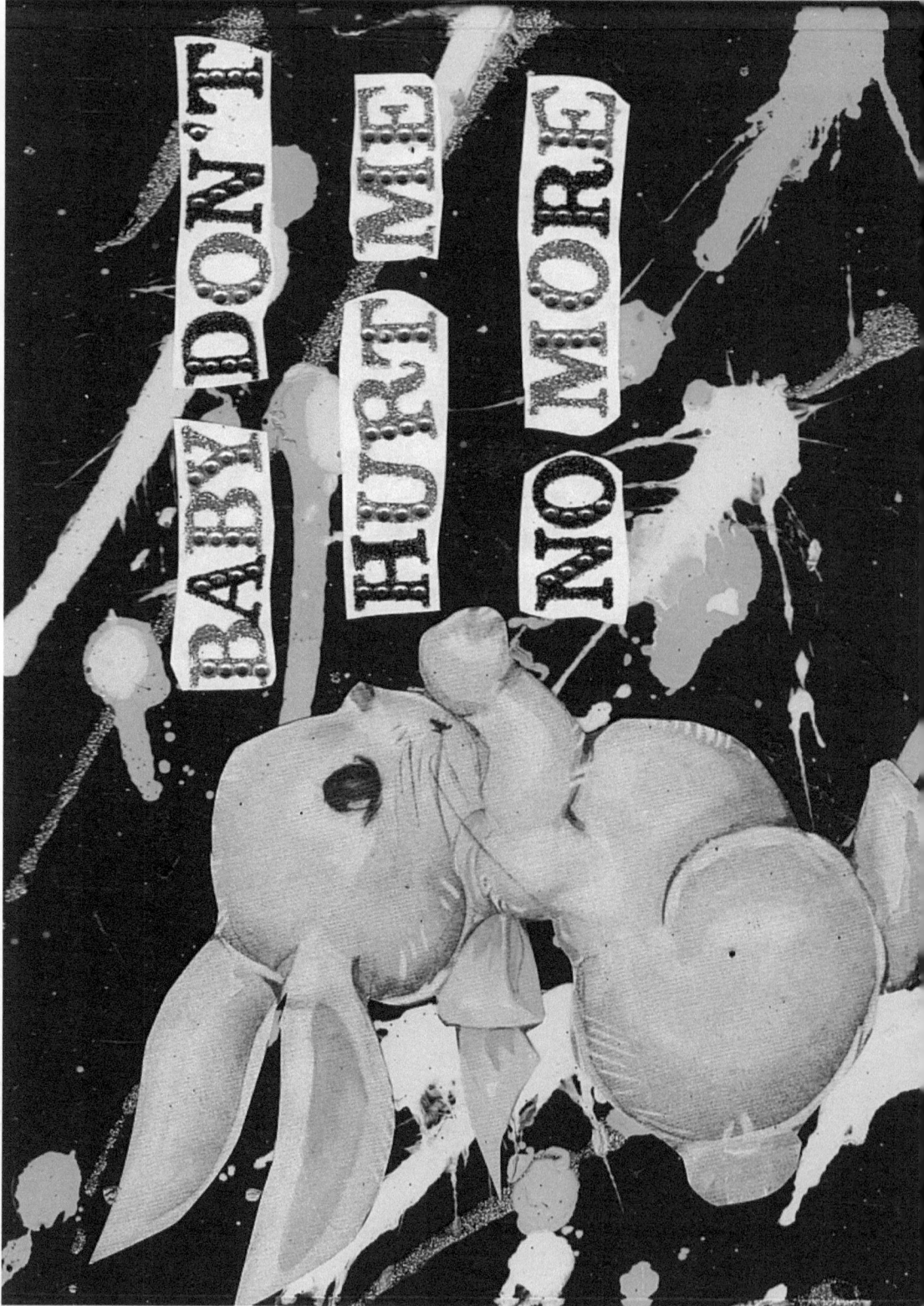

I'd Like To Join The Party But I Was Not Invited.

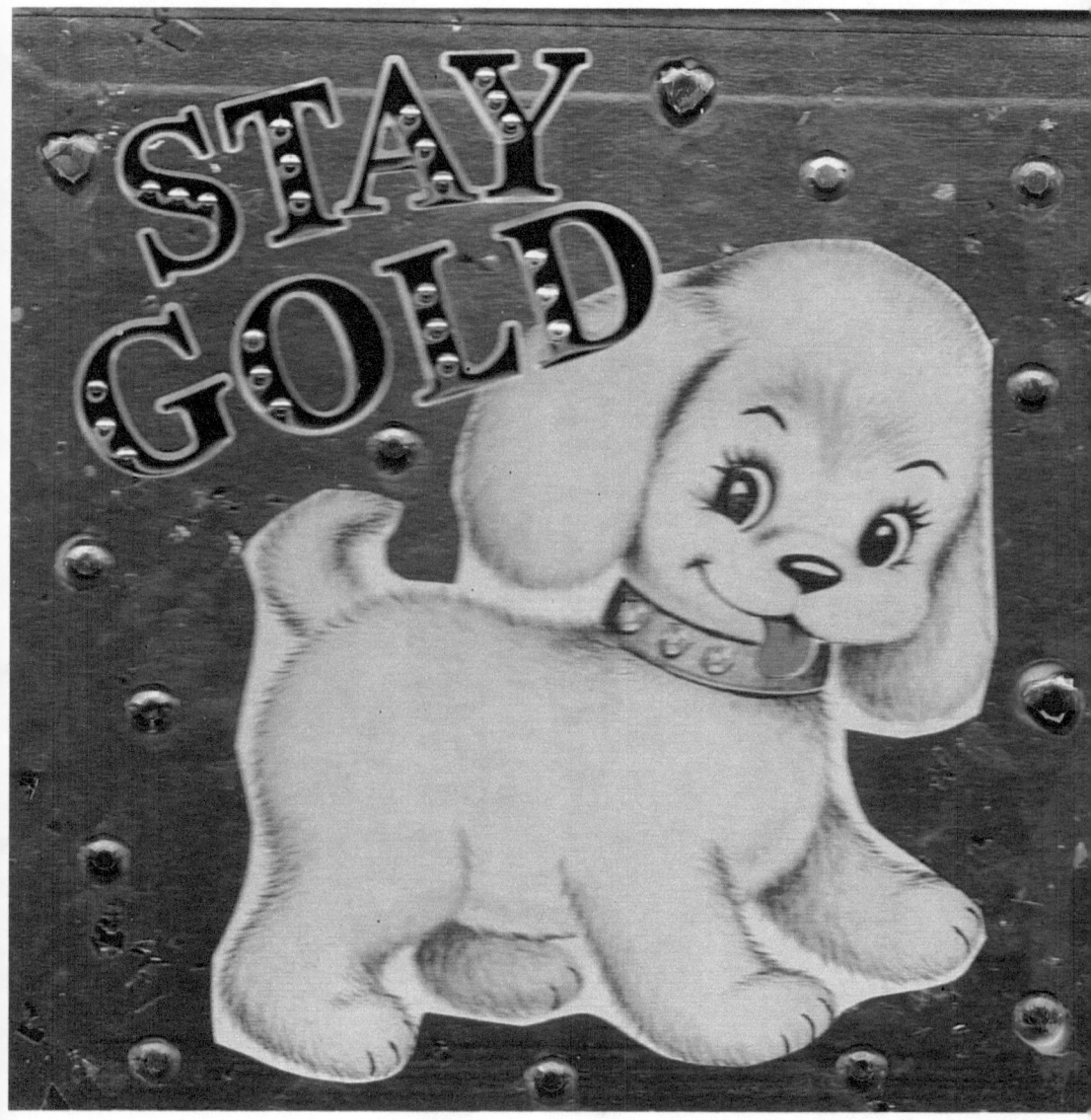

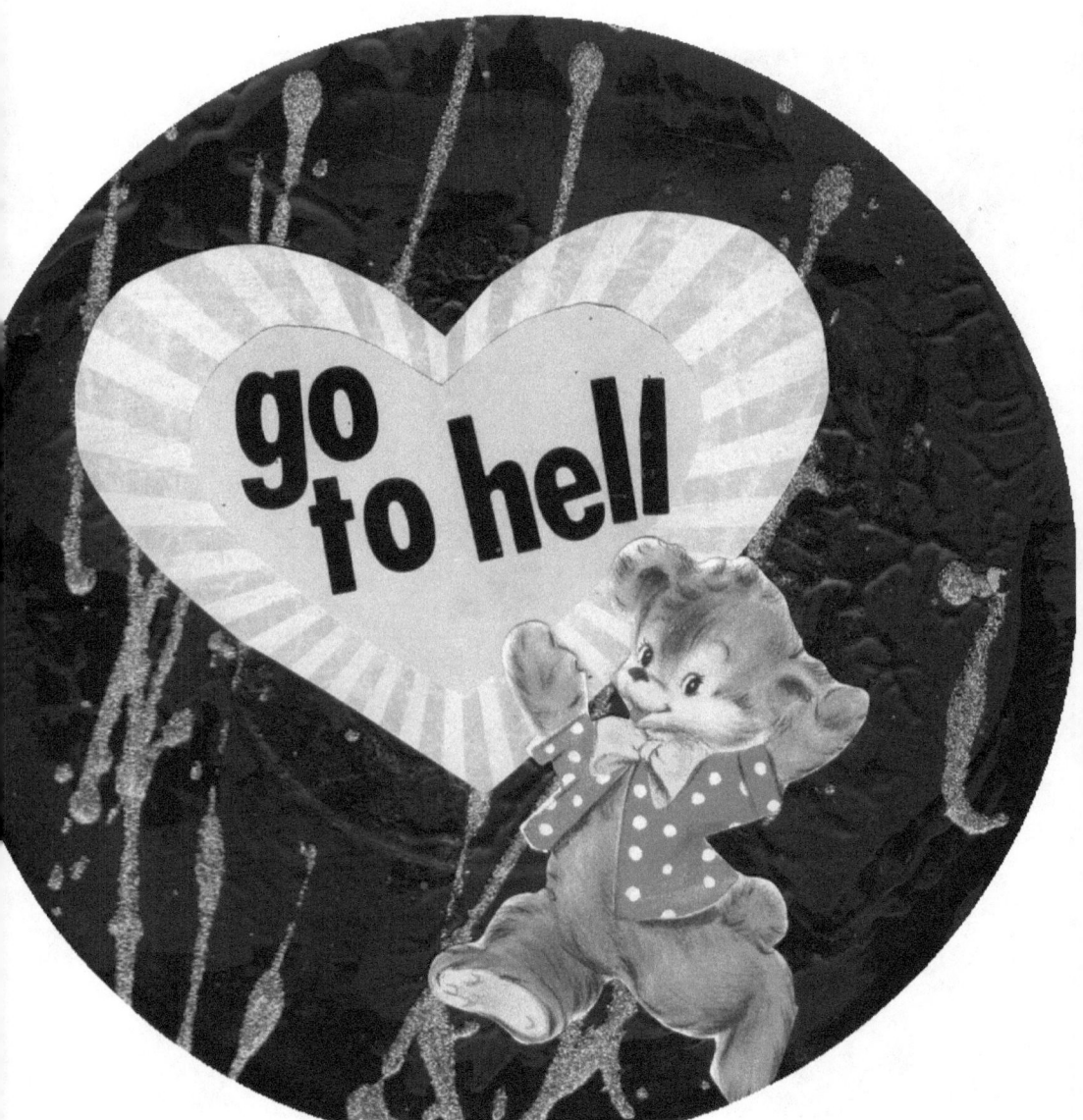

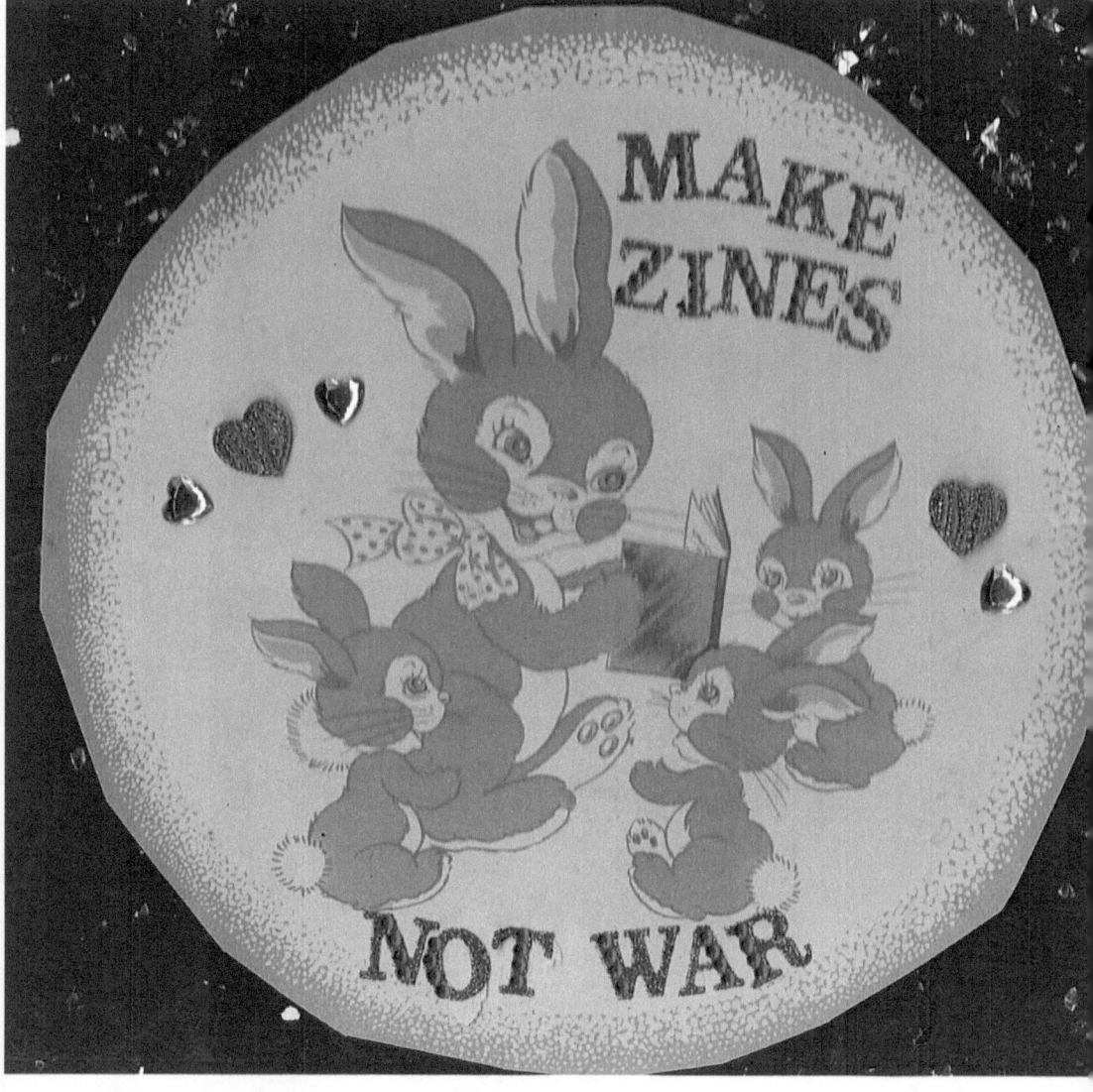

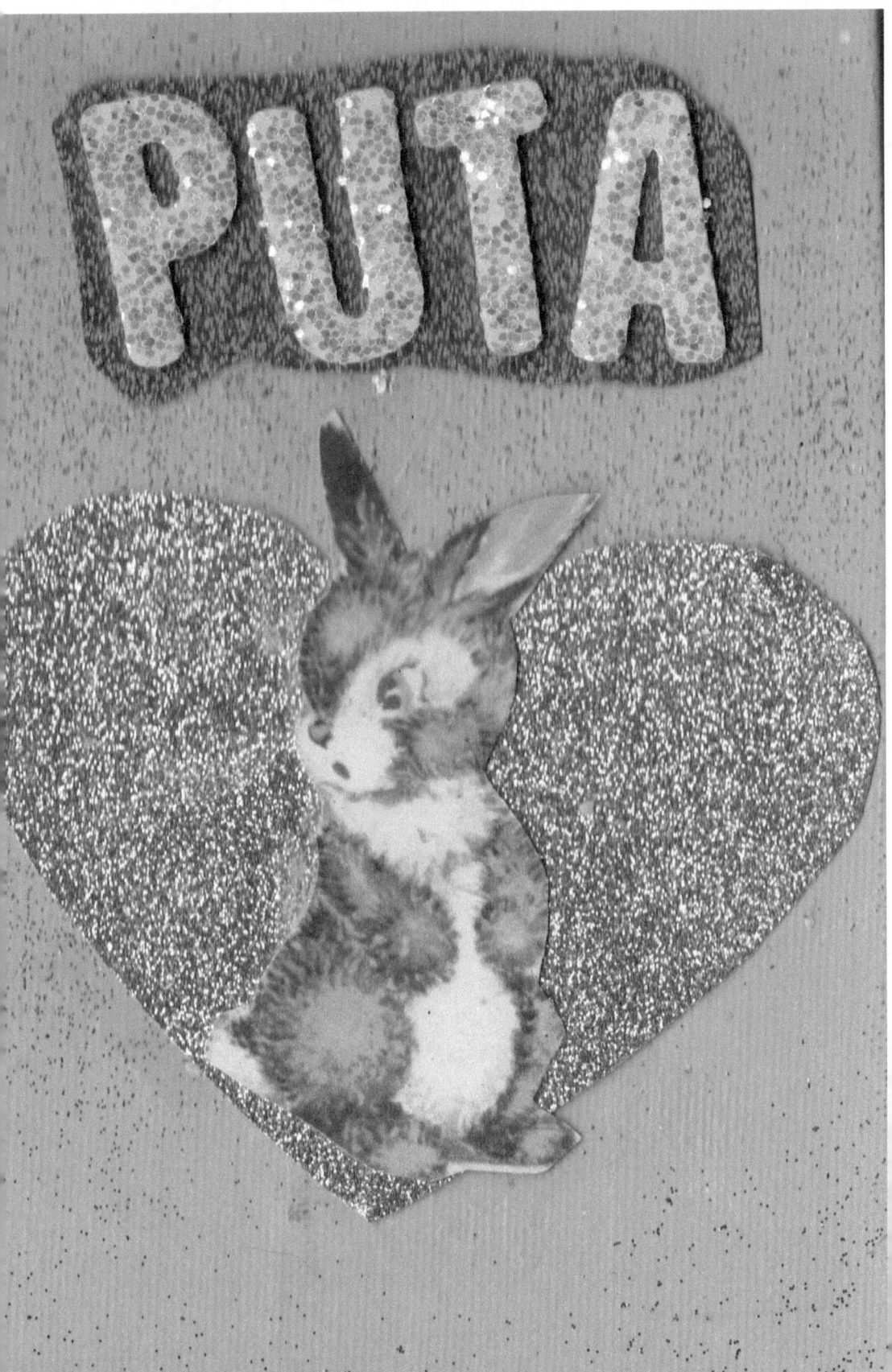

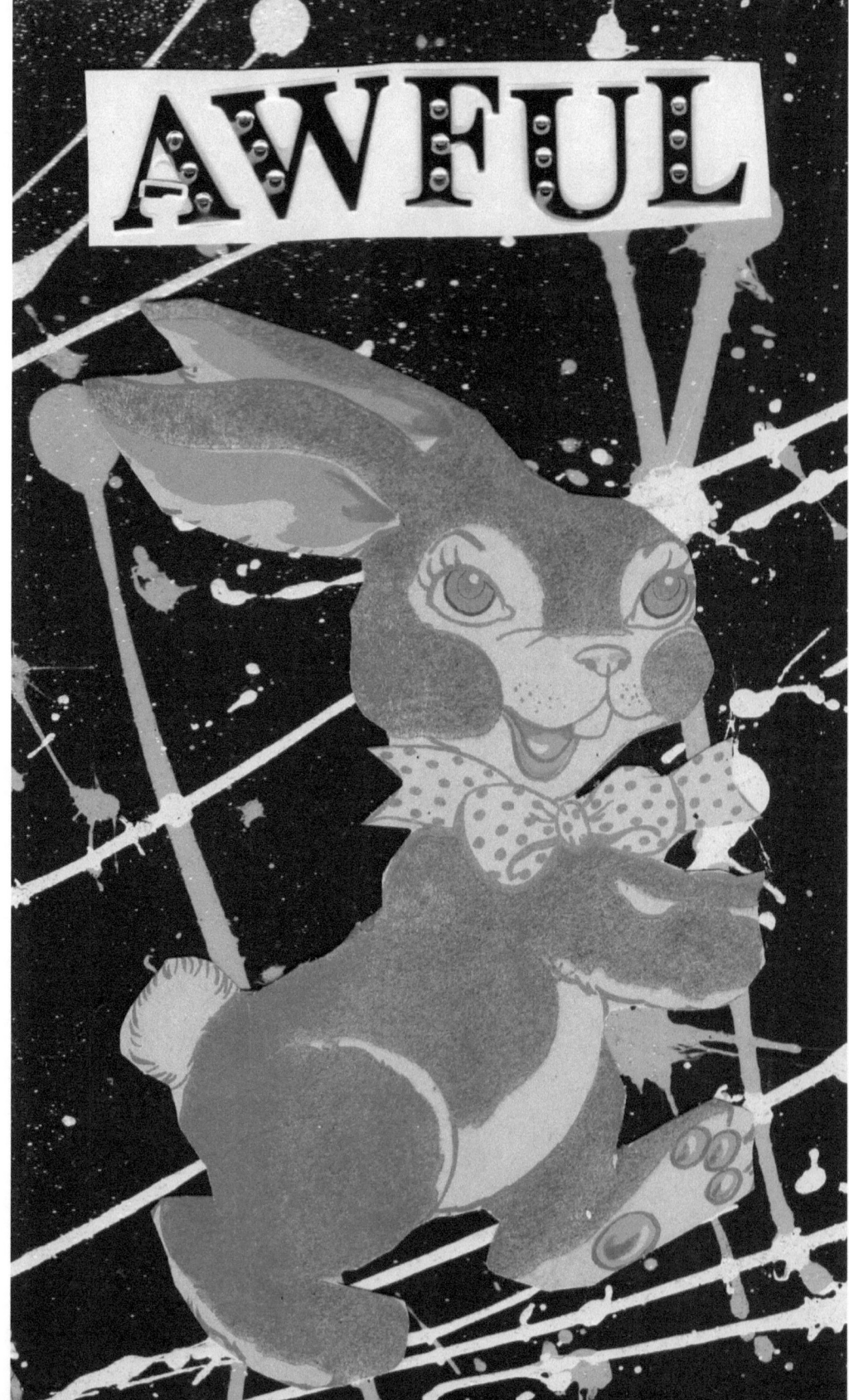

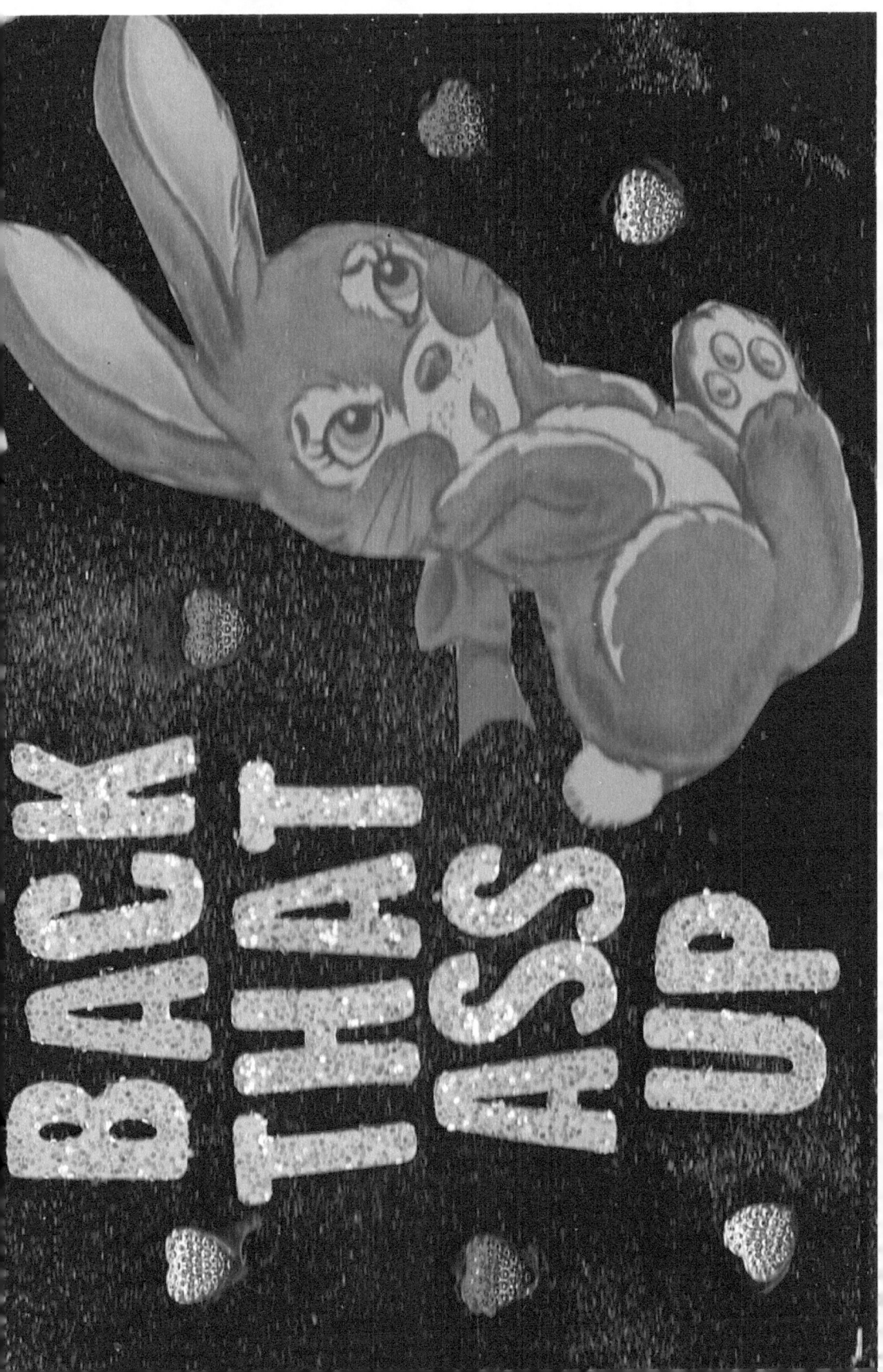

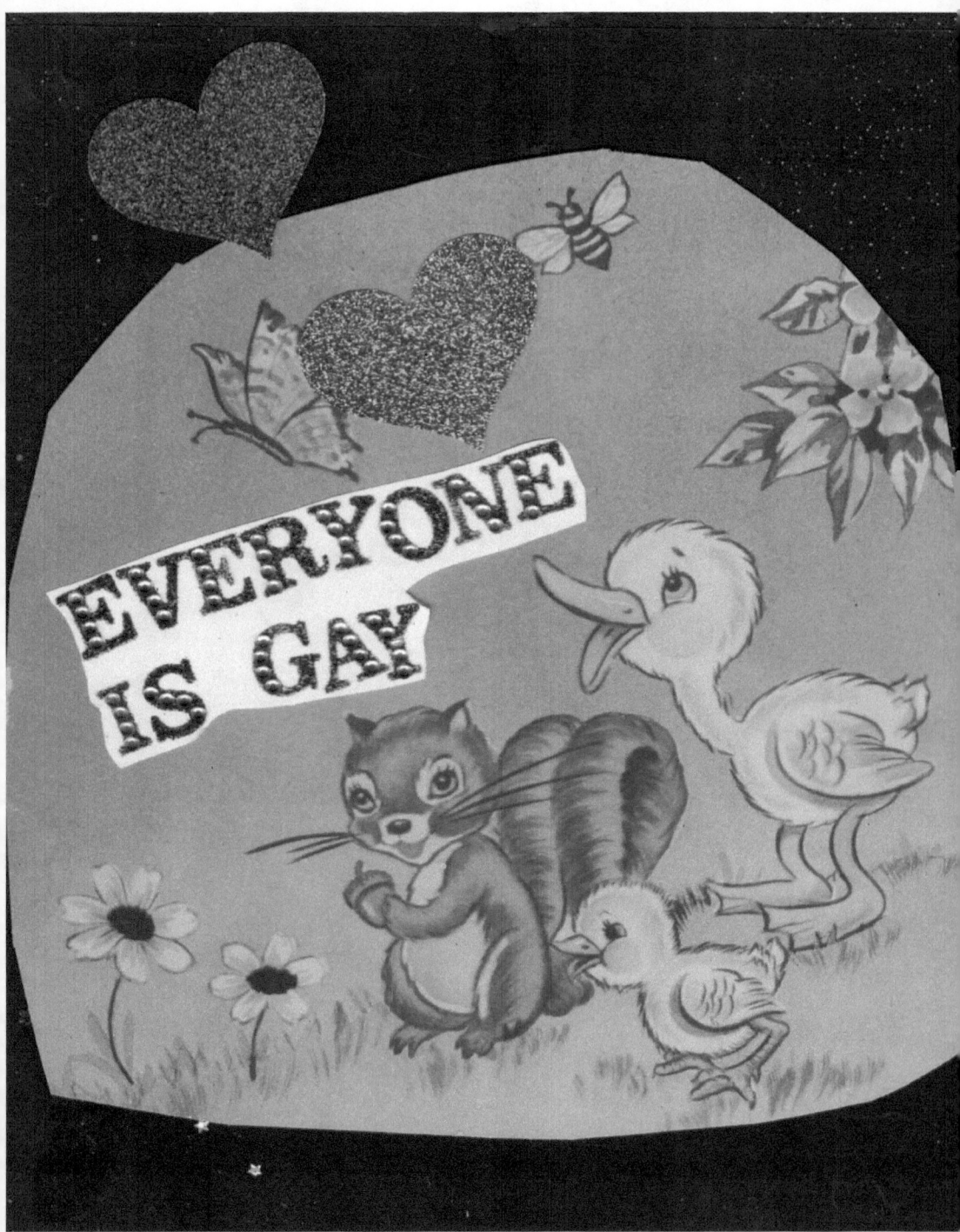

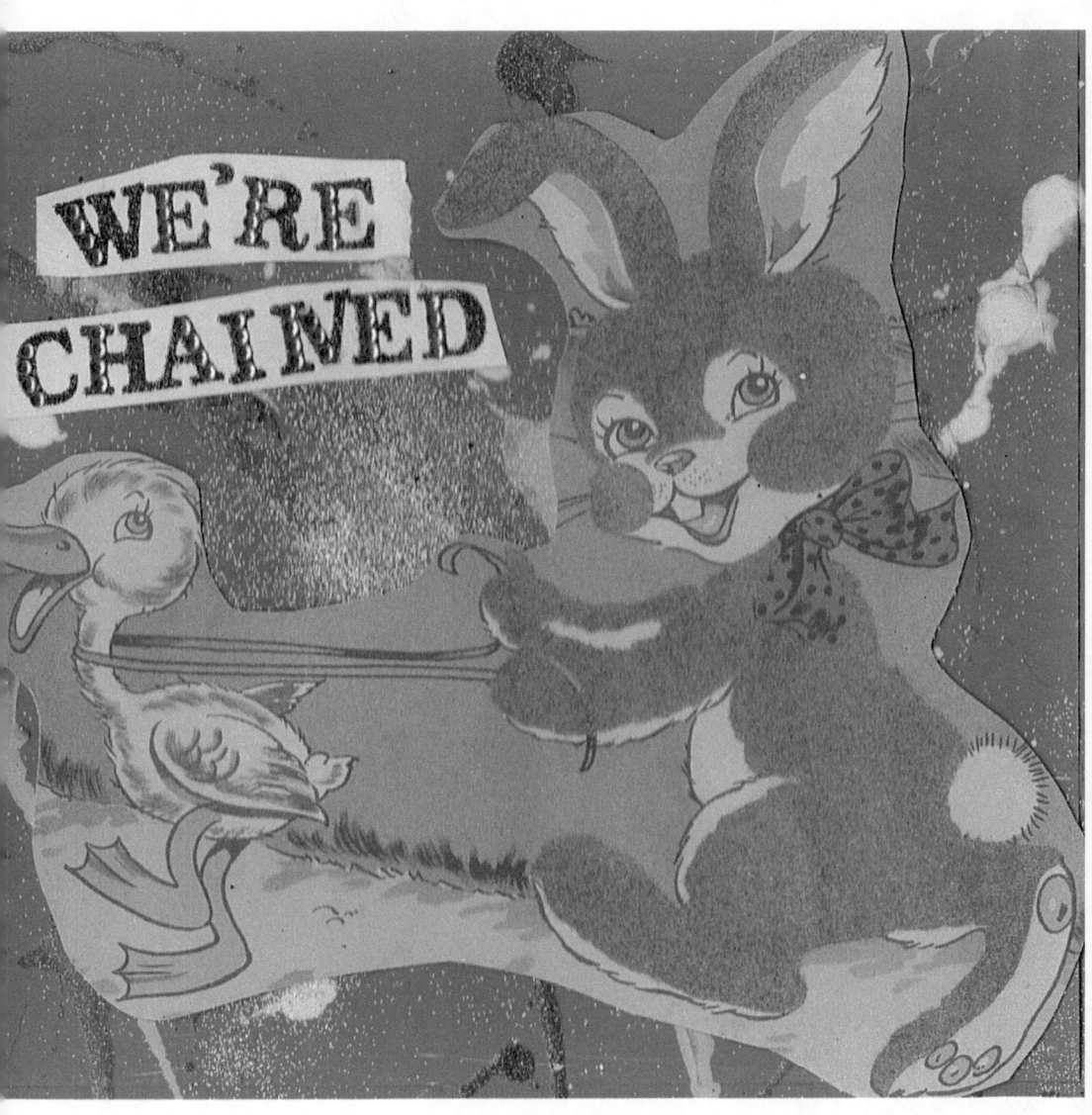

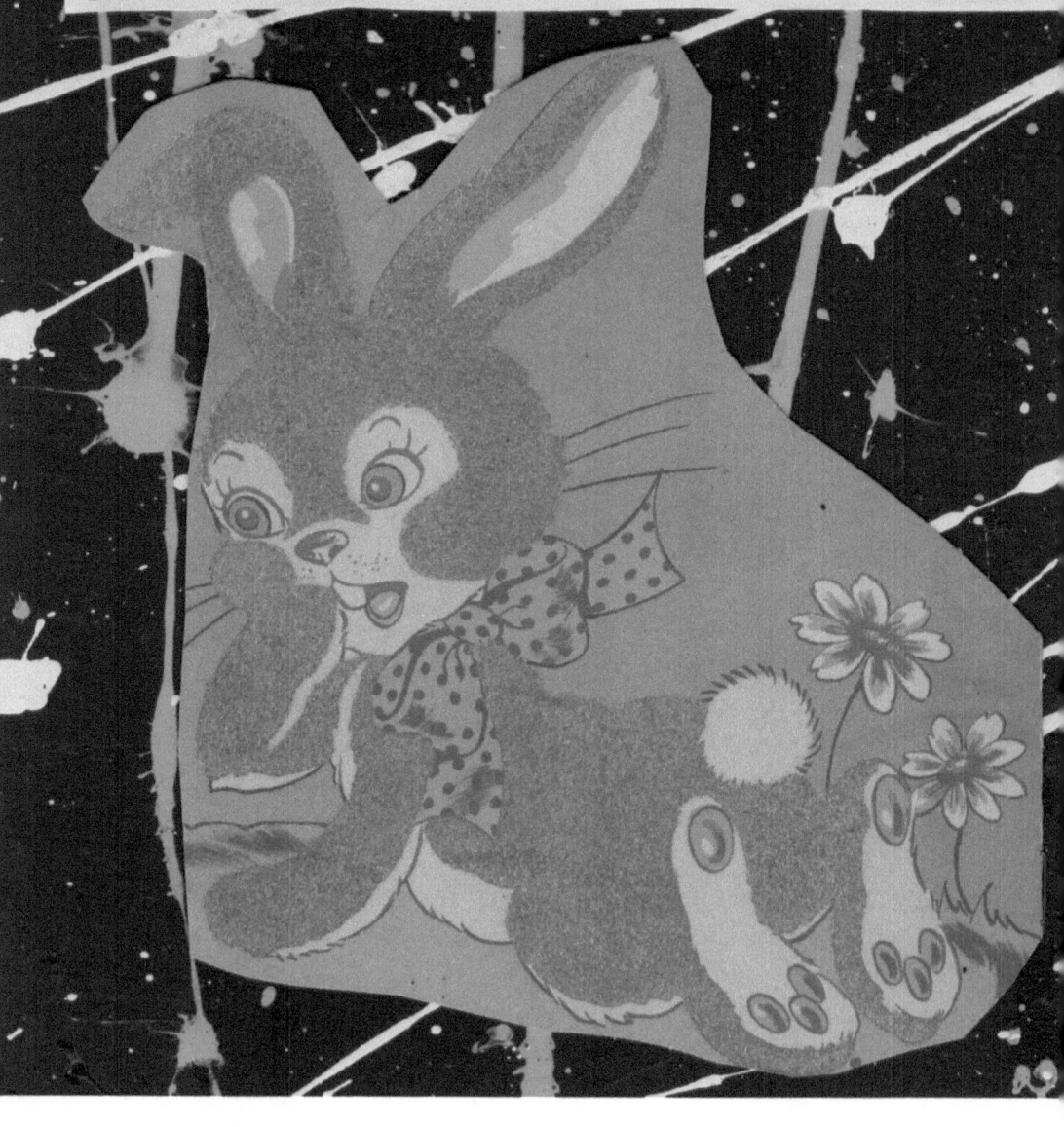

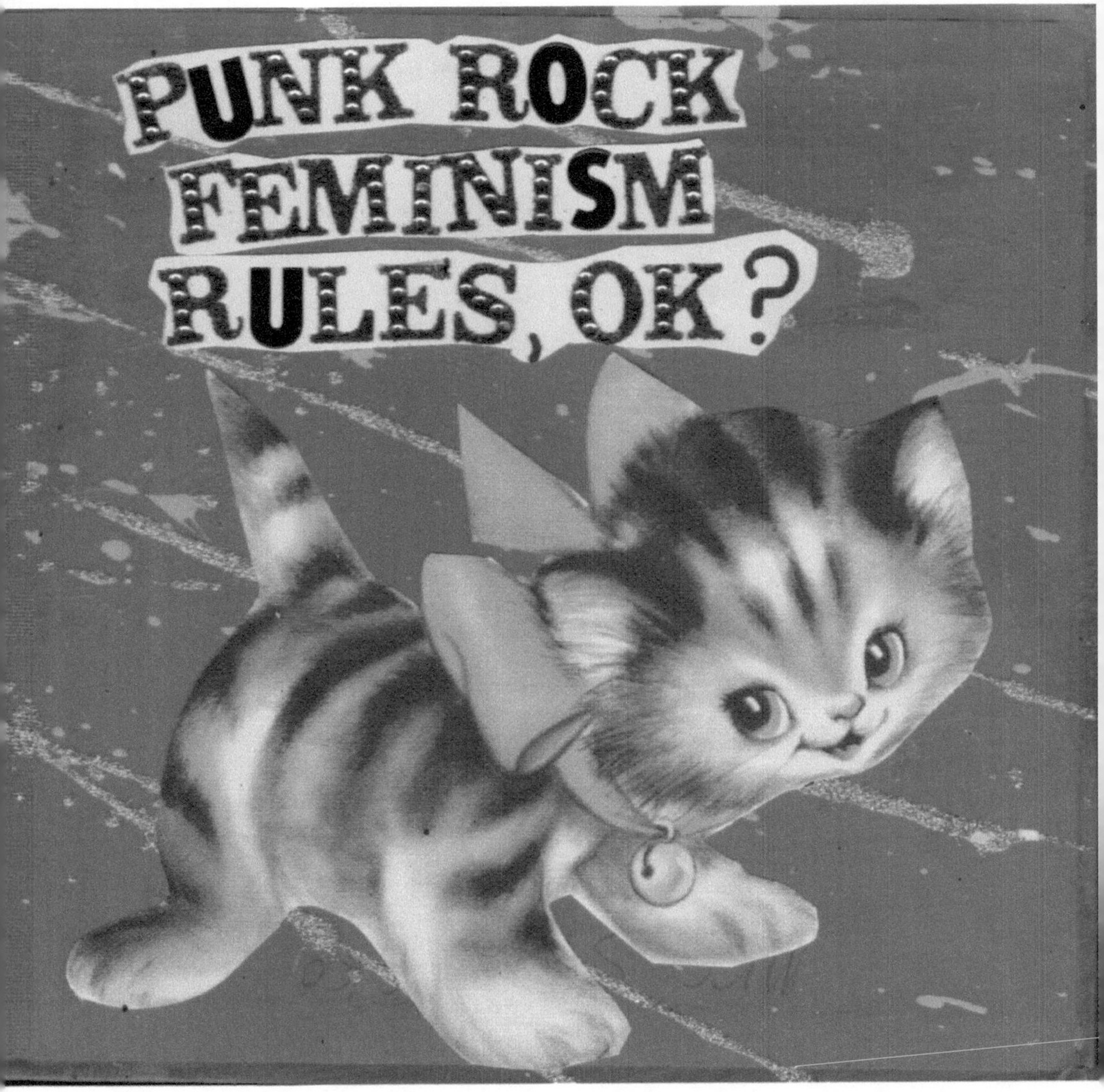

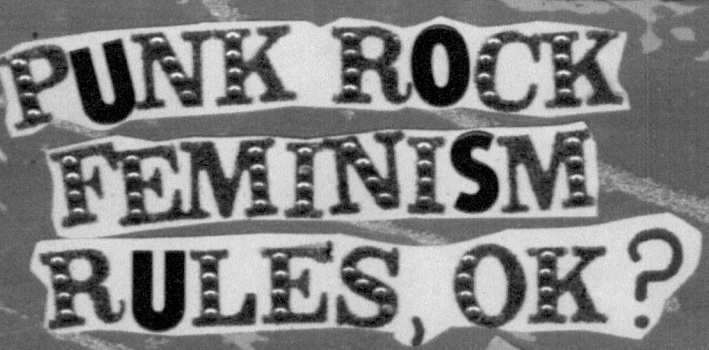

www.ingramcontent.com/pod-product-compliance
Lightning Source LLC
Chambersburg PA
CBHW030908180526
45163CB00004B/1756